Today's Tyrants

Responding to Dyson Heydon

Today's Tyrants

Responding to Dyson Heydon

Edited by Damien Freeman

The Kapunda Press

THE KAPUNDA PRESS

(An imprint of Connor Court Publishing in association with the PM Glynn Institute)

Edited by Damien Freeman

Fellow of the PM Glynn Institute, Australian Catholic University

The Kapunda Press is an initiative of Connor Court Publishing in association with Australian Catholic University's public policy think-tank, the PM Glynn Institute. The Institute is named after one of the founding fathers of the Australian Constitution — Patrick McMahon Glynn, who edited the *Kapunda Herald* from 1883 to 1891.

CONNOR COURT PUBLISHING PTY LTD

PO Box 7257

Redland Bay QLD 4165

sales@connorcourt.com, www.connorcourtpublishing.com

Cover image: Detail from a Wall Painting, Drake House, Melbourne (St Patrick's) Campus, Australian Catholic University.

ISBN: 9781925826227

Cover design by Ian James

"Christians living in the Roman Empire before Constantine made Christianity the empire's official religion faced little risk of being thrown to the lions if they practiced their religion in secret; it doesn't follow that Rome did not persecute Christians . . ."

Judge Posner, *Muhur v Ashcroft*

CONTENTS

The Inaugural PM Glynn Lecture on Religion, Law and Public Life

Responding to Dyson Heydon

FOREWORD

John Fahey

I was tremendously impressed when I heard the Honourable J. D. Heydon AC QC deliver the inaugural PM Glynn Lecture on Religion, Law and Public Life in Adelaide last year. Mr Heydon deftly combined his immense learning in history and the law in order to provide an insightful comment on public life in contemporary Australia and the threats that he sees on the horizon for it.

As Chancellor of Australian Catholic University, I was delighted that the University's public policy think-tank, the PM Glynn Institute, was able to establish this annual lecture and to recruit a speaker of such eminence to deliver the inaugural lecture. This volume represents the next phase of the Institute's endeavour. Not content with having given Mr Heydon a platform from which to start an important conversation, the Institute has now commissioned a set of responses to the lecture to continue the conversation that was commenced in Adelaide last year.

This volume showcases the work of scholars within the Faculties of Arts, Law, and Theology and Philosophy at the University, as well as that of scholars at other academic institutions with which the Institute has established a working relationship, including the University of Notre Dame Australia and the University of Melbourne. The Institute has also solicited contributions from thinkers with wide-ranging affiliations beyond academe, including the Sydney Institute, Catholic Social Services Australia, *The Australian*, the Centre for Independent Studies, and the Victorian Bar.

Nuturing a conversation between the University's scholars and figures in public life, commentators in the press, Catholic agencies, and other universities is central to the PM Glynn Institute's role as a public policy think-tank. These sorts of conversations about public affairs are vital for the flourishing of our society, and this volume will go a long way in stimulating one such conversation. I commend the Institute for the auspicious moment that is the publication of the first book in this series, and I look forward to reading the next one, which will contain responses to the second lecture, which I had the privilege of hearing Dr Jesse Norman MP deliver earlier this year.

The Hon. John Fahey AC

Sydney,

1 September 2018

INTRODUCTION

Damien Freeman

Drake House is the vice-chancellor's residence on the Melbourne (St Patrick's) Campus of Australian Catholic University. The townhouse, originally named 'Mon Sejour', dates from 1883. Following extensive renovation and restoration, it was renamed in 2011 for the distinguished development economist, Professor Peter Drake, who served as the University's first vice-chancellor. The restoration process saw the removal of wallpaper that was probably put up when the building had functioned as a boarding house. Beneath the wallpaper in the central hall and stairwell, a most remarkable discovery was made. Located just below eyelevel, a frieze depicting numerous scenes from mediaeval life has been painted directly onto the surface of the wall. It runs all the way around the ground-floor hall, and up to the second-floor landing, where it culminates in a wedding feast. Little is known about this charming mural, but is seems likely that it would have been commissioned for the building's original incarnation as a Victorian gentleman's residence fit for the elite of the Federation generation.

The image on the dustjacket covering this volume is taken from the frieze. It depicts members of the mediaeval lord's family making merry with lute, pipe and harp, while their lord sits apart, resisting their frivolous musical diversions, all the while determinedly keeping his head down in contemplation of the book he is reading. This somehow seems a most fitting image to select for the cover of a work so intimately connected with J. D. Heydon QC. In the distant past, when I was giving Mr Justice Meagher a Hebrew lesson, we got distracted from the passage that we were reading about Sampson in the Book of Judges, and got to be talking about his brother judge, Dyson Heydon. The exact connection that Roddy Meagher saw between Dyson and Sampson, I cannot remember. I can remember, however, Roddy explaining to me, "Dyson does not appreciate music, which is good, because it proves that no-one is perfect."

The Honourable John Dyson Heydon was born on 1 March 1943 in Ottawa, Canada, to the Australian diplomat, Sir Peter Heydon CBE, and his wife, Lady (Muriel Naomi) Heydon. He was educated in London, Rio de Janiero and Wellington, before attending Sydney Church of England Grammar School and St Paul's College in the University of Sydney. He graduated in 1964 with a Bachelor of Arts degree with first-class Honours and the University Medal in History. Later that year, he proceeded to the University of Oxford, where he read for a second BA in law at Keble College, as the Rhodes Scholar for New South Wales, and shared the Martin Wronker Prize for the top first-class Honours degree in law in 1966. He then undertook a Bachelor of Civil Law degree and was awarded the Vinerian Scholarship for the highest first-class degree in that course in 1967.

From 1967 to 1973, Mr Heydon was a fellow and tutor at Keble College, Oxford, during which time he also lectured on evidence and trusts at the Inns of Court School of Law. In 1969, he served as a visiting lecturer at the University of Ghana, before being appointed professor of law at the University of Sydney, at the age of twenty-nine. He taught and published on equity, evidence, commercial and company law, and restrictive trade practices, and served as dean of the university's law school in 1978-79.

He was admitted to the New South Wales Bar in 1973 and was appointed Queen's Counsel in 1987. He practised at the Bar from 1979, as a member of the Eighth Floor of Selborne Chambers, until his appointment to the New South Wales Court of Appeal in 2000. He was sometime editor of each of the *Australian Law Reports*, the *New South Wales Law Reports*, and the *Australian Bar Review*, and was a member of the Bar Council for five years from 1982.

He served as the forty-fourth Justice of the High Court of Australia from 2003 until 2013.

By Letters Patent issued on 13 March 2014, the Governor-General appointed him as a sole Royal Commissioner for the Royal Commission into Trade Union Governance and Corruption.

He is the author of numerous legal texts, including *The Restraint of*

Trade Doctrine (1971), *Economic Torts* (1973), *Case Book on Evidence* (1975), *Cases and Materials on Equity* (1975), and *Heydon and Donald on Trade Practices Law* (1978), and the editor of editions of such seminal texts as *Cross on Evidence* (1970) and *Meagher, Gummow and Lehane's Equity: Doctrines and Remedies* (2002).

He was named as a Companion of the Order of Australia in the Queen's Birthday Honours List for 2004, and awarded the degree of Doctor of Laws (*honoris causa*) by the University of Sydney in 2007. As if this were not honour enough, ten years later, in 2017, he was named as the inaugural PM Glynn Lecturer on Religion, Law and Public Life.

The PM Glynn Lecture on Religion, Law and Public Life was established by Australian Catholic University's public policy think-tank, the PM Glynn Institute, to honour the contribution that its namesake, Patrick McMahon Glynn, made to Australia, both as one of the founding fathers of the Commonwealth, and as a prominent writer, lawyer and parliamentarian. This annual lecture invites an eminent person to address an important question at the intersection of religion, the law and public life with a view to enhancing the quality of discussion about important matters of public policy.

Dr Michael Casey, the foundation director of the PM Glynn Institute, wrote in the preface to a pamphlet containing the inaugural lecture, "Glynn's own convictions about the importance of religion, law and public life powerfully informed the contribution he made in many areas, and as a distinguished jurist and scholar, Mr Heydon is particularly well-placed to reflect on the importance of these three critical dimensions of our life in common."

The inaugural lecture was entitled "Religious 'toleration' in modern Australia: the tyranny of relativism", and it is reproduced at the beginning of this volume. The lecture commences by introducing the "elite of the Federation generation" and reflecting on their deference to religious authority. They are contrasted with the "modern elites", who, it is suggested, seek to exclude any role for religion in Australian public discussion. Two recent incidents are discussed, which are said to exemplify the modern elites' transition from indifference to religion to a form of anti-clericalism. Drawing on Peter Kurti's *The Tyranny of Tolerance*, it is suggested that the modern elites' tendency towards anti-clericalism has not only allowed them to associate themselves with anti-religious violence, but also with a failure to appeal to reason. Their demands for "tolerance" are revealed to be demands for "unconditional surrender" and unconditional acceptance of their chosen creeds. In making such demands, it is argued that they overlook the role of courtesy and reason in public discourse and civil society. Their creed is said to embody a modern ideal of liberalism in which there is neither a place for persuasion of those with whom one disagrees, nor tolerance of them. As a form of secular liberalism, the modern elites' creed is shown to have its origin in Christianity, by reference to Sir Larry Siedentop's *Inventing the Individual*, which traces the roots of liberalism back to values revealed by the advent of Christ. And yet, it is claimed, the modern elites not only despise and seek to marginalise the Christian religion that introduced the notions of the inherent value and fundamental equality of all human beings, which are central to any form of liberalism, but they go further in rejecting the cultural tradition of Christianity. Although it is conceded that the exercise of public power by the legislature and the judiciary has not yet significantly threatened the interests of religious people and their institutions, it is suggested that the modern elites might soon resort to the force of law. The lecture concludes with the admonition that, although for the time being it is only through conduct such as bullying and ridicule that the elites seek to prevent public expression of religion, this might be a sign of darker times to come.

This lecture was one of several contributions to discussions about public policy in Australia that the PM Glynn Institute has initiated in its first two years. Other contributions may be found in papers that it has published which set out the Institute's position on key issues. These include *Chalice of Liberty*, which discusses options for protecting religious freedom, and *Upholding the Big Ideas*, which provides options for constitutional recognition of Indigenous peoples. The purpose of the current volume is not, however, to advance the Institute's position on any matter concerning public policy. Rather, its purpose is to stimulate thoughtful and respectful discussion about the issues raised in the inaugural PM Glynn Lecture. The Institute regards its role in encouraging such discussion as no less important than its role in advancing policy proposals. Twelve men and women drawn both from the academy and beyond it have participated in this first discussion, and the Institute is grateful to all who have contributed to this volume by kindly giving of their time and intellectual pursuits to write essays that develop some aspect of the lecture in a new and original way.

The collection of responses begins with three broadly historical essays that investigate themes raised by the lecture. Frank Brennan discusses the attitude of the Federation generation's elite to religion, particularly in the debates at the constitutional conventions held in the 1890s, and charts a similarly respectful discussion in the proceedings of the 1988 Constitutional Commission and the 1998 Constitutional Convention, before observing that twenty years later such public debate has become less tolerant and respectful, particularly where religion is concerned. Anne Henderson observes that whereas argument and persuasion were legitimate tools for enabling men to transcend the sectarianism of Australian society a century ago, these tools cannot be deployed so effectively in contemporary Australian society, which has been freed of sectarianism, but burdened by virtue-signalling and groupthink intolerance, which threaten freedom of speech in a way that cannot easily be combatted by argument and persuasion. Paul Kelly chronicles the debate in 2017 and 2018 leading to the legalisation of same-sex marriage, and demonstrates the way in which the conduct of this debate allowed a commitment to non-discrimination to squeeze out any meaningful place for a commitment to religious freedom in Australian political debate.

These are followed by three essays that offer different approaches to analysing the lecture's central preoccupation with religious freedom in Australia. M. A. Casey takes the reference in the lecture to "the current war on religious faith" as a departure point for thinking about what the undermining of freedom of religion says about the state of a liberal society, such as Australia, and why it matters that a society such as ours should continue to affirm the value of freedom of religion and freedom of conscience. M. J. Crennan provides a comparative study of the law's approach to freedom of religion in Australia, under section 116 of the Commonwealth Constitution, and in the United States, under the First Amendment to the American Constitution. Peter Kurti offers an analysis of the intellectual and political developments that threaten to undermine freedom of religion in Australia, in an essay that is an edited and revised excerpt from his book, *The Tyranny of Tolerance: Threats to Religious Liberty in Australia*, published by Connor Court in 2017.

The lecture's conception of the modern elites and their agenda provides a departure point for the next three essays. Hayden Ramsay identifies the need for conservatives to develop a new narrative that can provide an alternative to the relativistic narrative embraced by the modern elites, and he finds in the lecture the elements of such a new narrative. Shireen Morris offers a warning to conservative elites, who, she argues, may well be guilty of the very conduct for which they condemn the modern elites, and suggests that the radical centre offers an alternative to the stalemate between the modern elites and the conservative elites. Michael Ondaatje offers a different perspective on the elites, which largely supports the lecture's analysis, but suggests there are further dimensions to the current problem that are not unpacked in the lecture.

The volume concludes with two essays that investigate themes on which the lecture only touches. Sandra Lynch provides a philosophical analysis of topics relating to relativism, tolerance and morality which underpin some of the central claims that the lecture makes about the current challenges for public life. Finally, Catherine Renshaw provides a fitting conclusion to the collection, with an essay that offers some thoughts about the place of reason and courtesy in the future of legal education, and how improved pedagogy might help remedy some of the contemporary disorder to which the lecture speaks.

Although Patrick McMahon Glynn was born in Galway, Ireland, and immigrated to Victoria, he did not enjoy any real success until he established himself in the mining town of Kapunda in South Australia. And so it is with that State's capital city of Adelaide that he is largely identified today: the city where he served in the South Australian House of Assembly for many years; where he attended the first meeting of the 1897 constitutional convention; whose residents he represented in the federal parliament between 1901 and 1919; and where he died in 1931. Thus, it is fitting that the inaugural lecture was delivered in Adelaide on 17 October 2017 as a tribute to its namesake. It was generously hosted by His Grace the Archbishop of Adelaide at the Monastery in Urrbrae, at the foot of the Adelaide Hills and in the Parish of St Paul of the Cross, Glen Osmond, home of the Passionist Community since 1896.

THE INAUGURAL PM GLYNN LECTURE ON RELIGION, LAW AND PUBLIC LIFE

Religious 'Toleration' in Modern Australia: The Tyranny of Relativism

J. D. Heydon

Today, 17 October, is the feast day of St Ignatius—not the famous St Ignatius of Loyola, but the Bishop of Antioch. He is said to have been the first person to use the words 'catholic church' in writing as meaning the active church that is identical across all Christian congregations. One does, however, suspect that a close search of the New Testament would reveal cognate usages before his time. The career of St Ignatius was marked by a stress on the real humanity of Christ, and therefore on the actuality of the physical sufferings of Christ. He had an ardent desire for martyrdom as a means of sharing the Passion of Christ. His fame rests on seven letters he wrote after his arrest during a persecution of the church in Antioch. He wrote them as he travelled in chains under military escort to Rome. He reached Rome in about AD 110, as the non-politically correct are for the time being permitted to call that year. That was in the reign of that *beau idéal* of the so-called 'good' Emperors, the Emperor Trajan, successful soldier and promiscuous drunk. St Ignatius's desire for martyrdom was met when he was condemned to the wild beasts in the Roman arena. The career of St Ignatius of Antioch is not entirely irrelevant to what follows, but for the moment let us move to the happier subject of Patrick McMahon Glynn.

It is a great honour to have been invited, on this auspicious day, to deliver the inaugural Glynn Lecture, and to do so in his adopted home, Adelaide. He certainly deserves to be remembered in this way. I regret my inability to do justice to him. His life shows what a career lay open to Catholic talent both in nineteenth-century Ireland under the Protestant Ascendancy and in the four decades on either side of 1900, as the Australian colonies moved to Federation and towards independence. If he met sectarian prejudice, it did not slow him down. The son of a small

3

town shopkeeper passed from what is now Blackrock College, to Trinity College, Dublin, to the Middle Temple, to the Irish Bar, at the age of twenty-five to the Victorian Bar, to a brief period selling insurance and sewing machines, to practising law in South Australia. Then he entered political life, as an advocate of the once-popular but now forgotten views of Henry George—that there should be only one tax, a land tax. Taken as a whole, his career reveals him to be what might be called a radical conservative with socialist tinges, strongly influenced by his ardent Catholic faith.

In short, he was difficult to pigeonhole. In that career he supported female suffrage and suffrage reform generally, free trade, land nationalisation, the nationalisation of public utilities and other monopolies, Federation and Irish home rule. He supported the miners in their strike at Broken Hill in 1892. But his attractiveness to the Labor cause was doubtless diminished by his opposition to legislation restricting Chinese immigration to South Australia. He had great powers as a publicist and as an orator. He gained a great reputation for independence of thought, for culture, for learning and for rock-like integrity. He served several times in the South Australian Parliament. He served in the Federal Convention in 1897-98. He then served in the federal House of Representatives from 1901 to 1919. He also served three times as a federal minister. Well-informed opinion holds that if he had retained his seat after 1919, there might never have been a Bruce-Page government or a Bruce prime ministership, but rather a Glynn prime ministership. That is because, great statesman though Stanley Melbourne Bruce turned out to be, by the early 1920s he had much less experience than Glynn. But for present purposes let us remember the opening words of the Imperial Act which brought our Constitution into being:

> Whereas the people of New South Wales, Victoria, South Australia, Queensland and Tasmania, humbly relying on the blessing of Almighty God, have agreed to unite in one indissoluble Federal Commonwealth under the Crown . . .

To Glynn is traditionally assigned the authorship of that reference to humble reliance on the blessing of Almighty God.

Those words reflected what the elite of the Federation generation saw as fundamental. They do not reflect what modern elites think. The public voices of modern elites are not humble. They conceive themselves to have entitlements and rights, not blessings. And they do not feel any gratitude to Almighty God for their entitlements and rights. This lecture centres on the desire of modern elites to exclude any role for religion in Australian public discussion—and perhaps any role for religion at all in any sphere, public or private.

Any statement or other conduct which modern elites do not like is instantly made the subject of a demand that there be an apology. Modern elites consider that what one does not condemn one must be taken to accept. Modern elites have failed to understand that that places them in a difficult position. Some little time ago a particular point of view was publicised with the words: "Burn churches, not gays". The level of taste which is integral to this contribution can be gauged from the remembrance it summons up—surely inevitably and probably intentionally—of the fact that the last organisation in the West with any power to burn places of worship was the Nazi regime, and the fact that that regime moved very quickly from burning Jewish synagogues in November 1938 to burning those who attended those synagogues from 1942 onwards—in their millions.

Let us look at a second charmless incident. More recently vandals daubed on the walls of a Baptist church the words "Crucify 'No' Voters". The level of taste involved can be gauged from its deliberate and blasphemous allusion to a central element of Christian belief. This would not easily be seen by some elements in modern elites, who seem to waver between the contradictory contentions that Christ never existed, or that Christ was never crucified, or that the Roman soldiers who attempted the crucifixion behaved with such incompetence that Christ merely fell unconscious and never actually died on the Cross.

Does not the failure of modern elites to condemn these two examples of sub-human behaviour indicate an acceptance by the elites of their propriety and validity?

A related catchcry commonly now heard is "Why don't religious people stop forcing their opinions on everyone else?" This call for what in Germany in the 1940s would have been called a compulsory inner emigration will be discussed later below.

These phenomena highlight an aspect of modern elites—the relativism of their beliefs and their conduct. It is all right for one element of public opinion to call for the physical destruction of places of worship and the death of those who worship in them. That is treated as merely routine, apparently fit to pass without comment. But it is not seen as all right for those who worship to state publicly the beliefs they hold, and to argue, whether on narrowly religious, or ethical or utilitarian grounds, for or against particular policy positions under general debate. It is all right for the elite to support a particular point of view, but intolerable for anyone else to oppose it. That is what modern elites call 'tolerance'.

Until recently the approach of modern elites to religion was one of indifference. It is easy to understand how this came to be. The horrors of life in earlier times made it understandable that human beings were strongly attracted to seeking consolation in religious faith and in the hope of a better world after life in this world ended. We forget the extent to which some types of prosperity have become much more common in the West. And we forget how fast this has happened. A century ago the great Dutch historian J. H. Huizinga commenced his work *The Waning of the Middle Ages* as follows, in a chapter entitled "The Violent Tenor of Life":

> To the world when it was half a thousand years younger, the outlines of all things seemed more clearly marked than to us. The contrast between suffering and joy, between adversity and happiness, appeared more striking. All experience had yet to the minds of men the directness and absoluteness of the pleasure and pain of child-life. Every event, every action, was still embodied in expressive and solemn forms, which raised them to the dignity of a ritual. For it was not merely the great facts of birth, marriage, and death which, by the sacredness of the sacrament, were raised to the rank of mysteries; incidents of less importance, like a journey, a task, a visit, were equally attended by a thousand formalities: benedictions, ceremonies, formulas.

> Calamities and indigence were more afflicting than at present;
> it was more difficult to guard against them, and to find solace.
> Illness and health presented a more striking contrast; the cold
> and darkness of winter were more real evils. Honours and riches
> were relished with greater avidity and contrasted more vividly
> with surrounding misery. We, at the present day, can hardly
> understand the keenness with which a fur coat, a good fire on
> the hearth, a soft bed, a glass of wine, were formerly enjoyed.[1]

In the century since Huizinga wrote those words, the contrast between the painful environment of past ages and the gluttonous and sensual milieu of the present has become far more marked. Now indifference based on rising wealth is insidiously damaging to religion. Prosperity has proved a graver foe than persecution. As the world we are in becomes more attractive, the less need is there for contemplating the possibility of some other more perfect world and the less adherence there is to a strict morality.

Lord Acton said that "the moral law is written on the tablets of eternity". Apart from laying down the moral law, religion asks two questions. What is the nature of humanity? What is the destiny of humanity? It tries to transcend the trivial and the worldly. It looks for windows into another world. It may not stress a tragic vision of life. But it does try to stress a serious vision of life. To those satisfied with the pleasures of this world, now so freely available, questioning and searching of these kinds is of no interest.

But members of modern elites are moving away from mere indifference. They are embracing a fanatical anti-clericalism. Some want to destroy faith itself. We know there have been recent persecutions in the Middle East of a kind and on a scale that have not been seen for centuries—rarely under the Ottomans until their treatment of the Armenians, not much under the states which succeeded the Ottoman Empire. Now, however, mass murders and threats of mass murder are disrupting and scattering communities which have lived peacefully in the Middle East for a very long time in harmony with their neighbours. We must hope that never happens in Australia. But something which, though less severe, is equally uncompromising is emerging in Australia. Among the elites is developing a hostility to religion which has not been seen in the West since the worst excesses of the French Revolution, or at least the vengeful premiership of Émile Combes in the early 20th century. The hostility is demonstrated least against Hindus and Buddhists—for they are neither numerous nor highly visible. It is also not much demonstrated against Muslims, despite the threat and actuality of terrorist outrages, perhaps because the Muslim vote is the key to winning and losing parliamentary seats. It is beginning to be demonstrated against Jews. Their numbers are low, but those parts of the elites which respond to electoral hatred for the State of Israel are drifting back into an anti-Semitism which one had thought had been purged from Western life by the horrors of the Second World War and the persecution of Jews in Communist eastern Europe and Russia after 1945. No allowance is made for the appalling dilemmas facing Israeli leaders, surrounded as they are by a sea of Muslim hate. And hostility is increasing markedly against Catholics. One of the aphorisms of the great parliamentary leader of the German Centre Party, Ludwig Windthorst, is becoming true again: "Anti-Catholicism is the anti-Semitism of the intellectuals". But no Christian denomination seems to be exempt from the new de-Christianisation campaign.

Now it is evil to invite anti-religious violence. It is also evil to damage the property of religious institutions. To fail to denounce those evils is to associate oneself with them. The case for the elites is weakened not only by their association with those evils. It is also weakened by their failure to appeal to reason. There is among us here tonight the Reverend Peter Kurti, a licensed Anglican priest interested in the place of religion in Australian public life. He has recently written a remarkable book entitled *The Tyranny of Tolerance: Threats to Religious Liberty in Australia*. I owe a debt to it. For some of his themes underlie this address. In that book he argues that traditionally liberalism aimed to protect individuals against the encroaching power of the state. But this type of liberalism has been replaced. The new liberalism calls for the enervation of religious faith and religious practice. It sees faith as something which is at best an individual subjective profession of taste—a sort of hobby, harmless enough, but only if practised in private. Instead real tolerance extends only to those who are alleged to be victims of discrimination. He says:

> In truth, however, this tolerance is not 'open-mindedness'. It is a form of moralistic relativism concerned with elevating the rights and interests of any who are perceived to be victims of discriminatory or marginalising behaviour.
>
> Tolerance in the name of relativism has, indeed, become its own form of intolerance. We are commanded to respect all difference and anyone who disagrees can expect to be shouted down, silenced or, often, branded a racist. Everyone must be 'tolerant'.[2]

The modern elites are tyrants of tolerance. They say: "You must listen to what I am going to say. Then you must either praise my virtue or shut up. Because if you try to say you disagree and why, you deserve to be, and you will be, hounded out of all decent society." Thus the tyrants of tolerance pay lip-service, but only lip-service, to freedom of religion as a fundamental human right. Peter Kurti wants to defend freedom of religion. It can be destroyed by persecution in the manner of some Roman emperors or ISIS. It can be destroyed as well by the tactics of the tyrants of tolerance. Section 116 of the Constitution prevents the enactment of any Commonwealth law prohibiting the free exercise of religion. The tyrants of tolerance react to what religious speakers may say with orchestrated vilification, insults, derision, scorn, fake outrage and bullying mockery. That howling down can do as much to prevent the free exercise of religion as any law falling foul of section 116.

In short, modern elites do not demand tolerance. They demand unconditional surrender. They want absolute victory for an uncontestable dogma which is unchallengeable—or at all events is not to be exposed to the risk of challenge. The modern elites call for their creeds to be tolerated. Then they call for them to be compulsory. Then they want them to be exclusive. One small saving grace is that the contents of these creeds, dogmatically and absolutely stated though they are, do seem to vary from time to time.

9

This authoritarian claim overlooks the roles of both courtesy and reason.

In almost every way the last five or six decades have seen a massive change in courtesy, civility and mutual respect. Seats are not given up to the pregnant, the elderly and the infirm on public transport. Travellers are not given immunity from noise made by other travellers. Citizens are not free from noise made by their neighbours. Passersby in suburban streets are tending not to greet each other with the politeness of former times. Public violence and drunkenness is more common. Triviality and loutishness prevail in commercial life, and at all levels of public life from parliamentary processes to community debate.

But there is more wrong with the approach of the elites than discourtesy. Their approach disables them from—makes them incapable of—presenting their point of view, for what it is worth, properly. To shout is not to argue. To censor is not to reason. To bawl is not to engage in persuasion.

There is a form of persuasion associated with the eighth Duke of Devonshire. So far as he is known now at all, he is best known as the Marquess of Hartington, under which name he sat in the House of Commons for thirty-seven years until 1893. He had the unique distinction of being offered the prime ministership on three occasions, in 1880, 1886 and 1887, and each time refusing. The announcement in 1886 of Gladstone's plans to give home rule to Ireland caused the Duke to detach the Whigs from the right wing of the Liberal Party while Joseph Chamberlain led out the Unionist radicals from the left wing. As a much younger man the Duke had been the model for the leading character in Trollope's political novels, Plantagenet Palliser, Duke of Omnium. On 24 March 1908, he died with the words: "Well, the game is over, and I am not sorry." When the news reached the House of Commons that afternoon, the Prime Minister, Sir Henry Campbell-Bannerman, was ill and absent. He was a doomed man; he resigned ten days later, and within a month he too died. The duty of announcing the news of the Duke's death thus fell to Mr H. H. Asquith—then the Chancellor of the Exchequer, shortly to be Prime Minister. How was Mr Asquith to deal with the man whose fragmentation of the Liberal Party had kept it out of office for most of the previous twenty years? He paid him an elegant tribute—and a handsome one. He said that the Duke was "almost the last survivor of our heroic age". The Leader of the Opposition, Mr A. J. Balfour, the Prime Minister before Campbell-Bannerman, attempted to explain the source of the Duke's stature, in a speech which was in its day famous:

> I think of all the great statesmen I have known the Duke of Devonshire was the most persuasive speaker; and he was persuasive because he never attempted to conceal the strength of the case against him. . . .

> What made the Duke of Devonshire persuasive to friends and foes alike was that when he came before the House of Commons or any other Assembly, he told them the processes through which his own mind had gone in arriving at the conclusion at which he ultimately had arrived. Every man felt that this was no rhetorical device, but that he had shown in clear and unmistakable terms the very intimate processes by which he had arrived at the conclusion which he then honestly supported without fear or favour, without dread of criticism, without hope of applause. . . . In the Cabinet, in the House of Commons, in the House of Lords, on the public platform, wherever it was, every man said, "Here is one addressing us who has done his best to master every aspect of this question, who has been driven by logic to arrive at certain conclusions, and who is disguising from us no argument on either side which either weighed with him or moved him to come to the conclusion at which he has arrived. How can we hope to have a more clear-sighted or honest guide in the course we ought to pursue?" That was the secret of his great strength as an orator.

The point is that to expose and deal with the difficulties in one's case can be a passport to decisive intellectual success. It is not a technique employed by the elites. They will not concede any difficulty in their case. Or at least they will not concede any right in their opponents to expose any such difficulty.

Another curious feature of modern elites is this. They call themselves liberal and tolerant. Their 'liberalism' and 'tolerance' is the product of a long historical process. Modern liberalism in any genuine sense reveals several key characteristics—a belief in individual liberty, in the moral equality of individuals, in a legal system based on equal treatment of like cases, and in a representative form of democratic government. In the West, modern liberalism also goes further, in calling for massive public expenditure—on education at all levels, on public health, and on support for the aged, the poor, those incapable of work and those unable to get it. Opinions may differ on what the precise mix of these latter characteristics ideally should be, but there is no real difference about the former key characteristics.

How did this modern ideal of liberalism arise? Out of the very religion which is now the most despised—Christianity. From the time Christ walked the earth in Galilee trends began which though at varying speeds and in different ways and subject to various setbacks developed the modern age. The process has been traced in a fine book written by Sir Larry Siedentop, a man who, like Peter Kurti, is an old friend of mine. So my praise for both of them must be discounted for that fact. Sir Larry Siedentop was brought up in the United States. But he has lived and taught in England for five decades. His book is *Inventing the Individual: The Origins of Western Liberalism*. He points out that before the Greek and Roman republics emerged, society was based on families run by patriarchs. The Greek republics were in effect tyrannies or oligarchies. Rome was originally run by kings, then by a republican oligarchy, then by emperors whose power in the first and last resort rested on military strength. In these societies so-called 'citizens' were few in number. In different ways women, younger sons, slaves, captives and foreigners could enjoy only debased and limited roles. Even a genius like Aristotle viewed slavery as inevitable: "Some are free men, and others slaves by nature."[3] Thus natural inequality, and the natural superiority of the few over the many, were basic assumptions. The world was seen as dominated by many inscrutable deities and an uncontrollable and immutable fate.

The advent of Christ revealed different values. He showed a concern for the ill, the socially marginal, the outsider, the destitute. He opposed self-righteousness and hypocrisy. He had no concern to associate with wealth, power or celebrity. His associates were humbler. Many of them were women. He saw little children as heirs to the Kingdom of Heaven. He encouraged a search for the beam in one's own eye before identifying the mote in someone else's. He encouraged his followers not merely to love their friends and neighbours, but also to forgive their enemies. He urged them not to meet violence with violence. The social teachings of Christ were reflected, for example, in the monastic tradition later. Thus in the fourth century St Basil of Caesarea said: "It is God's will that we should nourish the hungry, give the thirsty to drink, and clothe the naked."[4] They live on in religious charities even to this very day.

But above all Christ taught that all human beings were equal before God, and all could enter the Kingdom of God.

His followers came to treat his life as a revolutionary and dramatic intervention of the divine into secular affairs. And they saw his role as going beyond the way his enemies saw him—as a rebel against unsympathetic religious leaders and Jewish puppets of Roman governors—to having universal significance for each individual human being. As Paul told the Galatians: "There is neither Jew nor Greek, there is neither slave nor free, there is neither male nor female; for you are all one in Christ Jesus."[5] Paul advocated relying on conscience and good intentions and abandoning the ritual behaviour of the ancient world and the Jews, with its mechanical following of rules and immemorial customs. He urged the exercise of free choice in accepting the gift of grace attained through faith in Christ. Salvation was a matter of personal decision to be resolved between each individual and God. In that sense all were equal. Those equal in the eye of God came to be seen as equal in the eye of the law. For this reason Siedentop asks: "Was Paul the greatest revolutionary in human history?"[6] And he states: "Through its emphasis on human equality, the New Testament stands out against the primary thrust of the ancient world, with its dominant assumptions of 'natural' inequality. Indeed the atmosphere of the New Testament is one of exhilarating detachment from the unthinking constraints of inherited social rules."[7]

So Tertullian said that Christ had done "one mighty deed . . . — to bring freedom to the human person".[8] In due course this attracted hostility from the Roman Empire. The persecutions of some Roman Emperors—not just failures like Nero or military dictators like Trajan or desperate rulers like Decius and Valerian trying to save a collapsing state, but objects of modern veneration like the supposedly civilised Marcus Aurelius—assisted the spread of Christianity. As Tertullian also said, the blood of the martyrs was "the seed of the church".[9] The process was perhaps aided, perhaps hindered, by the gradual conversion of that somewhat flawed figure, the Emperor Constantine, with his unfortunate identification of church and state. The last battle was fought by the Emperor Julian, who tried to revive paganism, but whose dying words were "Thou hast triumphed, Galilean." Yet even his goal was not to revive polytheistic paganism as it had been. Instead he wanted to create a new paganism with Christian influences, resting, like Christianity, on "the love of God and of fellow men", and asserting "charity" as its vocation. He saw the spread of Christianity as resting on "their benevolence to strangers, their care for the graves of the dead and the pretended holiness of their lives".[10] Even the great Councils of the fourth and fifth centuries prefigured the modern liberal world, as they tried to thrash out fundamental questions in long debates, like a nineteenth-century representative legislature.

Now the modern elites—the tyrants of tolerance—in seeking to marginalise or silence Christianity are not only rejecting the cultural tradition of Christianity. Not only are they rejecting a large part of the entire life and history of the nation—because Christianity is so integrated with the national life and history that to annihilate it is to destroy that national life, which can live only in memory. They are also rejecting that fundamental part of the Christian tradition which is the source of the modern world and of their own favoured position within it. They are doing it whether they realise it or not. To do that is to run a risk of returning at least in part to what the Christian tradition replaced. And what it replaced is rule by patriarchs, or aristocracies, or oligarchical castes, heavily based on slavery, involving the subjugation of women, captives and younger sons and not recognising the status of aliens. It is to drift towards the opposite of Christianity. Above all, the modern elites welcome tyranny. Why not? They are the tyrants of tolerance themselves, in tolerating only their mercurial views alone, even though those views change with the fickleness of fashion.

The Girondin leader Vergniaud said that the French Revolution, like Saturn, was devouring its own children. Like other Girondin leaders and many other revolutionary leaders from Danton and Robespierre down, he died under the guillotine. In Australia we see the reverse. The children of the Christian revolution, after denying that it was their father, are devouring the revolution.

Perhaps the last parts of the argument go too far. Members of modern elites would incredulously deny that their protected position owed anything to Christianity. But some of them would accept, perhaps, that that protected position owes something to classical secular liberalism. Liberalism endeavoured to create governmental structures which protected a private sphere of individual freedom. In that sphere, religious belief could survive. But some members of modern elites depart from their own origins in secular liberalism. By preventing any public expression of religious thought through ridicule and bullying, they tend to cause religion to wither away even in the private sphere. What can have no public expression will eventually cease to have any private existence. Thus the elites seek to destroy their inheritance from secular liberalism.

Sometimes the stance of the elites is defended by contending that there is no element of religious discrimination or persecution involved in requiring or inducing those of religious faith not to proselytise, manifest it publicly, or employ it as a source for the discussion of public issues, so long as they are at liberty to practise their faith in private. A bench of the United States Court of Appeals for the Seventh Circuit (Flaum CJ, Posner and Williams JJ) has denied this. The opinion, written by Judge Posner, pointed out that refugees are entitled to claim asylum on the basis of religious persecution even if they can escape the notice of their persecutors by concealing their religion. The Court said:

Christians living in the Roman Empire before Constantine made

> Christianity the empire's official religion faced little risk of
> being thrown to the lions if they practiced their religion in secret;
> it doesn't follow that Rome did not persecute Christians . . . [11]

Another argument which might be advanced for the elites, though it does not appear to have been, is that silencing religious persons by forcing them entirely out of the public arena is not discrimination, because it is not contrary to the *Racial Discrimination Act 1975*. Section 9(1) of the Act provides:

> It is unlawful for a person to do any act involving a distinction, exclusion, restriction or preference based on race, colour, descent or national or ethnic origin which has the purpose or effect of nullifying or impairing the recognition, enjoyment or exercise, on an equal footing, of any human right or fundamental freedom in the political, economic, social, cultural or any other field of public life.

That contains no reference to religion. And in the highly controversial section 18C, paragraph (1)(b) selects as a requirement for unlawfulness the doing of an act "because of the race, colour or national or ethnic origin of [a] person or of some or all . . . people in [a] group"—but not religion. If section 18C is to stay, why is religion not given the protection it affords? Perhaps this non-protection of religion is to be explained because the constitutional validity of section 9(1) probably can rest solely on section 51(xxix) of the Constitution. That gives the Commonwealth power to make laws about 'external affairs'. That has been read as including treaties. As a result of once controversial but now generally accepted decisions of the High Court, a statute giving effect to a treaty is valid under section 51(xxix) even though no other head of legislative power supports it. The treaty on which the Racial Discrimination Act is based defines "racial discrimination" as meaning "any distinction, exclusion, restriction or preference based on race, colour, descent, or national or ethnic origin which has the purpose or effect of nullifying or impairing the recognition, enjoyment or exercise, on an equal footing, of human rights and fundamental freedoms in the political, economic, social, cultural or any other field of public life".[12]

Again, there is no reference to religion. That may explain why the Act does not prevent religious discrimination.

It is true that section 351 of the *Fair Work Act 2009* prohibits employers from taking adverse action against an employee on religious grounds, subject to exceptions for certain actions taken against staff members of religious institutions. Outside that field religious persons are left without protection, unless it is to be found in state law. However, in the New South Wales *Anti-Discrimination Act 1977*, for example, there is no protection for religious activity as such.[13] There are protections for the incitement of hatred on the ground of race in section 20C(1). "Race" is defined as including "colour, nationality, descent and ethnic, ethno-religious or national origin". This leaves out religious origin other than "ethno-religious" origin. This entire issue of anti-religious discrimination and of protections against it may become important, of course, if the 'Yes' vote in the current plebiscite is in the majority.

So far as the exercise of state power by the legislature or the judiciary is concerned, it cannot be said yet to have threatened the interests of religious persons and their institutions as much as some of the elites would like. There are qualifications to that. One thinks of Archbishop Porteous. One thinks of the Victorian Court of Appeal's construction of some Victorian legislation.[14] The most immediate threat is from the conduct of the elites using methods other than the force of law itself. But a threat to religious institutions may not stop there. It may eventually come from the law itself. If it does, it may begin a trend which is likely to extend to many other institutions whom the elites and the state which they tend to dominate come to dislike. That is why even those who are not members of religious institutions and have no particular sympathy for them ought to fear the current war on religious faith.[15] But if the elites were able to proceed by force of law—whether by laws specifically directed against their religious enemy or by laws which have a damaging impact on that enemy unless protections are provided—some may think that the time for talking alone may have passed. Some may think that the time for resistance may have come. Some may see it as necessary to deliver sermons attacking unjust laws with sufficient power to threaten the life of governments, as Cardinal von Galen did against Nazi involuntary euthanasia, at the price of incarceration in a concentration camp. Some may see it as necessary to endure imprisonment and exile as Cardinal Mindszenty did for his stand against Communist oppression and expropriation in Hungary after 1945. Some may see it as necessary to endure imprisonment and expropriation, as thousands of priests and churches did for opposing Bismarck's anti-Catholic laws. Australian law now prevents any repetition of the fate of St Ignatius of Antioch. But perhaps once again some persecution—less brutal physically, but just as real—will be the seed of the church.

Let us return to the man honoured by this lecture. Had Glynn lived to see the days which a pessimist may consider to be coming, how would he have reacted to them? Probably with clear-headedness, but also with fire and passion.

RESPONDING TO DYSON HEYDON

1

A HISTORY OF RESPECTFUL DEBATE

Frank Brennan

In the inaugural PM Glynn Lecture, Dyson Heydon expressed strong concerns about "the desire of modern elites to exclude any role for religion in Australian public discussion—and perhaps any role for religion at all in any sphere, public or private." He rightly acknowledged that Patrick McMahon Glynn is "traditionally assigned the authorship" of the reference to humble reliance on the blessing of Almighty God in the preamble to the Australian Constitution. Heydon made two claims: "Those words reflected what the elite of the Federation generation saw as fundamental. They do not reflect what modern elites think." These two claims warrant closer examination.

Perhaps it was unsurprising that Heydon, speaking at the Australian Catholic University, gave added poignancy to these two claims, making some observations as a non-Catholic about contemporary anti-Catholicism within the elites. While asserting that a new "de-Christianisation campaign" was being waged against all Christian denominations, Heydon observed that "hostility is increasing markedly against Catholics", making Ludwig Windthorst's aphorism true once again: "Anti-Catholicism is the anti-Semitism of the intellectuals." Modern elites espousing individualism, personal autonomy and rational secularism have little tolerance or appreciation of organised religion, especially when the religious practitioners insist that tradition, authority, formal teaching, and hierarchy are relevant to religious thought and practice. It is no wonder Catholicism has been singled out for particular consideration, especially after the protracted papacy of Pope John Paul II who extended his universal teaching authority with a gruelling international travel agenda and a strict regime for dealing with internal dissent. In the wake of the Royal Commission into Institutional

Responses to Child Sexual Abuse, there has definitely been an increased scrutiny of the Catholic Church's governance arrangements in Australia, especially given its reach in providing such a range of education, health and welfare services, often when in receipt of government funds. Over 60 per cent of those persons alleging sexual abuse within a religious institution who sought private hearings at the royal commission claimed to have been abused in a Catholic institution. Despite having vast research resources, the royal commission was not able to demonstrate whether allegations of abuse per capita were more prevalent in Catholic institutions. The Catholic Church, like all other religious institutions, needed state assistance to address the plague of child sexual abuse. With state assistance, the church should be now more fit for purpose ensuring the safety and well-being of children in its care. One of the consequences of the royal commission has been a heightened mistrust of the Catholic Church even though its members are now represented at all levels of Australian society.

In nineteenth-century Australia, Catholics experienced regular adverse discrimination and exclusion. By 1995, the nation reached the stage that the swearing in of the new Governor-General by the Chief Justice in the presence of the Prime Minister, all three being Catholic, was hardly a matter of public comment. Recent media attention to Catholic leaders like Cardinal George Pell and Archbishop Philip Wilson has many citizens wondering if Catholics are once again a targeted group for adverse treatment in the public square.

The views of the citizenry on the place of religion in public life have always been contested and varied in Australia. At the time of Federation, the views of the elite over the place of religion in the public square and the due place of God in the Constitution were quite divided. Today, the views of modern elites are even more diverse, while the issue of religious freedom and its place in the national legal architecture is alive and well. The receipt of over 16,000 submissions to the Ruddock review on religious freedom in early 2018 demonstrates that the issue of religious freedom and its place in the national legal architecture is alive and well, and not altogether resolved. But that's because it never has been, and probably never will be.

On 22 April 1897, Glynn proposed a motion to the Australasian Federal Convention which was meeting in his hometown of Adelaide. His amendment to the preamble to the proposed Constitution required the insertion of just three words to suggest that it was by "invoking Divine Providence" that the people of the colonies had agreed to form the Commonwealth of Australia.[1] Convention delegates had received 42 petitions mainly from Christian groups seeking such an amendment. The largest petitioning group were 9,764 Presbyterians from Victoria. After Glynn's motion was lost by 11 votes to 17, Dr Rentoul from Ormond College, the Presbyterian College at Melbourne University, informed the Presbyterian Assembly of Victoria: "The mischief arose through a young Roman Catholic barrister being entrusted with the motion. He had not gone about it in the proper way."[2]

From the outset, there were members of the Federation elite who objected strongly to putting God into the Constitution. The original 1891 draft of the Constitution contained a simple provision: "A State shall not make any law prohibiting the free exercise of religion."[3] This provision remained in the drafts until 7 February 1898.

Immediately after Glynn had introduced his motion, the next speaker at the convention was Adye Douglas from Tasmania who commenced: "There is no doubt the sermon of the honourable gentleman would have been exceedingly interesting provided it had been given in another place, but why should we be called upon to invoke the Divine blessing I cannot understand. To do so is not the proper way of carrying out the religion idea at all. . . . Nothing can make religion more ridiculous than to have the form without the substance."[4]

The next speaker against the motion was no less a figure than Edmund Barton, the first Prime Minister and a founding member of the High Court of Australia. He told the convention: "I do not want a motion of this kind if it can be avoided, and I still think it would be a wise and gracious thing of my honourable friend not to press this motion. It is not with any feeling of irreverence that I say this, but because I think there are some occasions on which the invocation of the Deity is more reverently left out than made. There are, no doubt, a large number of electors who will go to the poll, when they vote to agree to this union, invoking Divine guidance. Still it is not our place to enquire, after the vote is over, into the hearts and minds of electors."[5] With the cleverness of the legal advocate, Barton asked: "We cannot say that the voters have invoked Divine guidance on the subject, even after the act has occurred; how much less can we say it now by way of prediction?"[6]

Barton was not anti-religious, but he thought that religion had a restricted space when it came to constitutional arrangements. He told the convention: "The whole mode of government, the whole province of the State, is secular. The whole business that is transacted by any community—however deeply Christian, unless it has an established church, unless religion is interwoven expressly and professedly with all its actions—is secular business as distinguished from religious business."[7] He concluded: "The best plan which can be adopted to a proposal of this kind, which is so likely to create dissension foreign to the objects of any church, or any Christian community, is that secular expressions should be left to secular matters while prayer should be left to its proper place."[8]

Glynn was greatly affected by Barton's strong intervention in the debate and thought it best that the matter not be further debated. He had brought the matter onto the floor of the convention at the urging of many petitioners and with the support of delegates some of whom had already left for home. He considered withdrawing his motion but was urged to press ahead. It was then put to the vote and was lost 11-17.[9] It is significant that the No voters included three future High Court justices: Barton, Higgins and O'Connor. Isaacs was the only future High Court justice on the floor to vote in favour, and he was not a Christian.

The matter was revisited a year later when the convention reconvened in Melbourne. On 8 February 1898, Henry Higgins unsuccessfully proposed that clause 109 be amended to include the Commonwealth as well as the States so that neither could make any law prohibiting the free exercise of religion. He proposed:

> A state shall not, nor shall the Commonwealth, make any
> law prohibiting the free exercise of any religion, or for the

establishment of any religion, or imposing any religious observance.[10]

Higgins was worried that if the preamble were to mention God, which seemed all the more likely, then the High Court in future might deduce an inferential power for the Commonwealth to make laws with respect to religion. He told the convention:

> If, as seems likely, an acknowledgement of the existence of the Almighty is inserted in the preamble of our Constitution, it will be necessary to re-assure a large number of good people that their rights with respect to religion will not be interfered with.[11]

Whether or not delegates agreed in principle with a mention of the Almighty, there seems to have been a general consensus that such a mention would help to get the Constitution over the line with the voting public. The lawyers at the convention disagreed about the likely effect of such a mention when it came to the Commonwealth's law-making power. Edmund Barton saw no problem as the Commonwealth would only have power to make laws with relation to matters specified in the Constitution. He told the convention: "I think it is quite clear that the Commonwealth will have no power to make any law regarding religion, even if no amendment such as that which has been suggested is agreed to."[12] He explained:

> The reason why the prohibition in the first draft of the Bill which was prepared in 1891 was confined to the states was that it could not, by any possibility, be concluded that it was necessary to extend such a provision to the Commonwealth, because no power was given to the Commonwealth to deal with the matter of religion. The position is the same now, and I do not think it will be substantially altered if the blessing of Divine Providence is invoked in the preamble. A preamble does not give power to anybody.[13]

Barton and those delegates who regarded any such provision as antiquated won the day. Higgins's amendment was negatived.[14]

On 2 March 1898, Glynn proposed another formula of words,

namely "humbly relying upon the blessing of Almighty God". In between the convention sessions, the delegates had received feedback and suggestions from the various colonial parliaments. Glynn said that his new formula "embodies the spirit of the nine suggestions in regard to this matter made by the various Houses of Parliament".[15] He told delegates, "The words I wish to insert are simple and unsectarian. . . . They will, I think, recommend the Constitution to thousands to whom the rest of its provisions may forever be a sealed book." There can be no doubt that the delegates had an eye to the consequences of the proposed amendment. Regardless of whether they thought it ideal to include a reference to Almighty God, they knew that such an inclusion would increase the prospects of a popular vote in favour of the proposed Constitution. Once again, Glynn waxed eloquently about the stamp of religion in contemporary Australia:

> It is this, not the iron hand of the law, that is the bond of society; it is this that gives unity and tone to the texture of the whole; it is this, that by subduing the domineering impulses and the reckless passions of the heart, turns discord to harmony, and evolves the law of moral progress out of the clashing purposes of life.[16]

Glynn was followed immediately by Henry Bournes Higgins who was later to be the author of the Harvester judgment prescribing a just minimum wage for a worker with an 'average' family seeking a frugal but dignified existence. Higgins told the Convention: "In Adelaide I voted against the insertion in the preamble of a form of words proposed by the honourable member, and it is with regret that I shall have to repeat that vote at the present time, because the Constitution contains no provision to obviate the bad effect which the insertion of these words will have."[17] Higgins said he would have no objection to the proposal "if I felt that in the Constitution we had a sufficient safeguard against the passing of religious laws by the Commonwealth".[18] Behind the scenes, he, Barton and some of the other lawyers at the Convention got to work crafting what would ultimately become section 116 of the Constitution which provides: "The Commonwealth shall not make any law for establishing any religion, or for imposing any religious observance, or for prohibiting the free exercise of any religion, and no religious test shall be required as a qualification for any office or public trust under the Commonwealth."

This provision drew on some of the language in the Constitution of the United States. It was included in Chapter V of the Australian Constitution which deals specifically with the States. Nowadays it is fashionable to invoke section 116 as some sort of constitutional entrenchment of the right to freedom of religion. But this was not the intention of the founders, and that's why it is included in a chapter dealing with the States. Higgins and Barton were worried that an acknowledgment of God in the preamble to the Constitution could provide a green light to the Commonwealth Parliament or Executive legislating or acting so as to impose some sort of religious observances whereas the founders thought this should remain the sole preserve of the States. It's not that they were concerned about the right of citizens to enjoy freedom of religion or freedom from religion. They simply saw religion and its public manifestations and limitations as matters for the States and not for the Commonwealth. They were worried that an 1892 decision of the Supreme Court of the United States, which then emboldened Congress to regulate trade on Sundays, could create a precedent with the Commonwealth trying to regulate civic life for religious reasons. Having traced the development of state constitutions in the original American colonies, the Supreme Court in *Church of the Holy Trinity v United States* had stated:

> If we pass beyond these matters to a view of American life, as expressed by its laws, its business, its customs, and its society, we find everywhere a clear recognition of the same truth. . . . These, and many other matters which might be noticed, add a volume of unofficial declarations to the mass of organic utterances that this is a Christian nation.[19]

Barton interjected when Higgins mentioned this Supreme Court decision: "That decision was followed practically by the decision that they were a Christian people." Higgins responded, "Yes. That decision was given in March or February, and four months afterwards it was enacted by Congress that the Chicago Exhibition should be closed upon Sundays, simply upon the ground that Sunday was a Christian day."[20] Higgins was worried that those who had organised the petitions to the Australasian Convention had not come clean with the electorate, admitting that an acknowledgment of God in the preamble might result in the Commonwealth Parliament legislating on matters such as Sunday trading. He told the convention:

> I think the people in Australia are as reverential as any people on the face of this earth, so I will make no opposition to the insertion of seemly and suitable words, provided that it is made perfectly clear in the substantive part of the Constitution that we are not conferring on the Commonwealth a power to pass religious laws. I want to leave that as a reserved power to the state, as it is now. Let the states have the power. . . . Each state at present has the power to impose religious laws. I want to leave that power with the state; I will not disturb that power; but I object to give to the Federation of Australia a tyrannous and overriding power over the whole of the people of Australia as to what day they will observe for religious reasons, and what day they will not observe for that purpose.[21]

Barton continued to be unimpressed with the whole tenor of the pre-ambular mention of God: "Just as I thought that the mover of the amendment in Adelaide, which amendment was defeated, might well not press it to a division, so I had hoped that we should have had no amendment of this kind moved here."[22] Like Higgins, he thought regulation of activities for religious reasons should be left to the States. Barton hoped there would not be a need for a division and a formal vote but if there were, he would vote against the motion as he did in Adelaide while "recognising the good intentions and high motives by which those who seek to introduce a declaration of this kind into the Constitution are actuated".[23] This was the true expression of the Federation elite. Not that they agreed on the need to place God in the Constitution, thereby affirming the place of religion in the public square, but that they conducted themselves civilly respecting the views and motivations of those holding contrary opinions. As debate on the preamble continued, Higgins circulated a substantive amendment which was the precursor to the ultimate section 116. It was the circulation of this amendment which allowed the Federation elite to agree without a division or vote that the preamble be agreed to, stating, "whereas the people" of the colonies "humbly relying on the blessing of Almighty God, have agreed to unite in one indissoluble Commonwealth".

Later in the day, Higgins introduced his substantive amendment which was the precursor to section 116 observing: "I simply want to leave things as they are. I do not want to interfere with any right the state has. I merely want to make it clear that, having inserted in the preamble of the Constitution certain words which, according to United States precedents, would involve certain inferential powers, there is no intention on the part of the Convention to confer even inferentially these powers on the Federal parliament."[24] It was here that he and Barton parted company. Barton fully expected that the rights of citizenship would be more respected and "the divorce between Church and state more pronounced" as the new Commonwealth progressed. Thus, if the States were to have power to make laws with respect to religion, why not the Commonwealth? Higgins's substantive amendment was carried by 25 votes to 16. Future High Court justices Higgins and Isaacs voted in favour, Barton and O'Connor against. There was no unanimous agreement of the legal elite about the place of God and religion in the Constitution at the birth of Federation.

Our founding fathers did not want the Constitution interfering with the powers of the States in relation to religion in any manner whatsoever. On consideration, they could therefore have omitted any clause relating to religion in the chapter on the States. But in view of the preamble and out of excessive caution, they wanted to ensure that the Commonwealth could never trespass into the field of law-making in relation to religion, even if the High Court were minded to deduce inferential power from the mention of God in the preamble.

Glynn has become the hero of religious liberty. At the end of the 1898 convention, Bishop J. R. Harmer, the Anglican Bishop of Adelaide, wrote to Glynn offering sincere congratulations on "a notable result, at which all true friends of religion cannot fail to rejoice".[25] Glynn was delighted that the convention closed on 17 March, St Patrick's Day, "the festival day of my native land which . . . is bound to me by ties of affection no more close than those living links which attach me to the country of my adoption, whose Constitution I have been privileged in helping to frame, and whose destinies I am proud to share."[26]

Dyson Heydon is not alone in thinking that Glynn's preambular amendment "reflected what the elite of the Federation saw as fundamental." It has become a received mantra. And to date there has been little enthusiasm for revisiting the provision. For example, the 1988 Constitutional Commission chaired by Sir Maurice Byers and including Gough Whitlam, Rupert Hamer and distinguished academic lawyers Leslie Zines and Enid Campbell received many submissions "from people expressing concern or protesting about what they thought was a proposal to remove from the preamble reference to reliance on 'the blessing of Almighty God' and 'unity under the Crown'." The Commission concluded that "for many people these notions are either the major underpinnings of our Constitution or at least cherished sentiments". This small constitutional elite were very deferential to public sentiment and had no desire to stir the possum: "It is clear that, in the same way as there was substantial support at the end of last century for the inclusion of reference to reliance on God, there would be considerable opposition to any attempt to remove the reference to God from the preamble."[27] The commission concluded that a revised preamble "could be a source of passionate debate which would be a significant distraction from other substantive and more important proposals submitted to the electors."[28]

On the first day of the 1998 Constitutional Convention, which considered whether and how Australia might become a republic, Senator Ron Boswell moved, and the Reverend Tim Costello seconded, a motion that the Convention commence each day with the same prayer as said in both houses of parliament each sitting day. Costello said that some of his best friends were atheists, "So to all the atheists here who wish to vote against it: you will remain my best friends."[29] Boswell conceded that there was a diverse range of delegates at the convention but urged agreement for daily prayer as "It's going to be a very important Convention that is going to have to come up with an outcome that is in the best interests of Australia".[30] There was no opposition voiced, and prayers were offered each day.

The convention set up a working group on the preamble and the transitional covering clauses of the Constitution. There were three subgroups within the working group set up to consider particular matters of concern including constitutional recognition of Indigenous Australians, constitutional recognition of citizens' rights and retention of the words "humbly relying on the blessing of Almighty God". Anglican Archbishop Peter Hollingworth, later to be Governor-General, convened the third subgroup. He reported to the convention a recommendation to retain Glynn's words noting, "This action will keep our Constitution clearly in line with nearly all other constitutions of nations in this region and beyond where reference is made to the Divinity as the source of all power and be a unifying statement for people of all religious faiths throughout Australia".[31] Without debate, the motion was carried by the working group and brought to the floor of the convention where the discussion was respectful.

Hollingworth was concerned that the Constitutional Centenary Foundation, of which he was a member, had already recommended that the reference to God be deleted. Referring back to the 1898 convention debates, Hollingworth said there was "strong demand for the inclusion of reference to Almighty God". He thought Sir John Downer who had joined Barton and O'Connor as the members of the Drafting Committee at the Convention, had best summed up the nineteenth-century debate when he said that "the Commonwealth will be from its first stage a Christian Commonwealth". Hollingworth conceded, "Clearly that is not the way things have worked out. We cannot claim that Australia is, ever has been or perhaps is ever likely to be—certainly not in our time—a Christian Commonwealth, but that does not imply that we should become a purely secular republic."[32] A touch melodramatically, the archbishop claimed, "If we were to delete that reference, we would stand with the

People's Republic of China alone among all the other nations in this region—and, indeed in most other parts of the world, —which include reference to God in the preface to the constitutions of their lands".[33] Christine Milne favoured a more inclusive term like "spiritual wealth". Pat O'Shane said she was "probably the most committed atheist in the chamber" but that she had no objection to retaining the words.[34] Glenda Hewitt suggested that God be placed in lower case.[35]

On the floor of the convention, the discussion about God in the preamble was very respectful of both the subject matter and the differing perspectives on same. The Reverend Tim Costello said:

> There has been quite a lot of debate about that, but I think that is a very refreshing value, particularly if we find a way of wording it which means students can appeal to their spiritual resources. In the face of crass materialism, oppressive materialism and everyone talking about the bottom line—as if that only ever can mean an economic bottom line—the value of referring to God, to spiritual reality, says that as Australians we affirm there are things more fundamental, that there is a dimension of life much more life-giving than simply the values that seem to be so dominant with the advertisers and mind benders today.[36]

Presenting the subgroup's suggestion to the floor of the convention, Hollingworth explained that "the word 'God' is to be understood in the generic sense as every man, woman and child understands him/her to be according to their own particular experience." He added, "I think that problem covers the issue!"[37] The 1998 convention agreed that, in the event of Australia becoming a republic, the preamble to the Constitution should contain a reference to Almighty God.[38]

Twenty years on, public disputation about all manner of things in the Australian public square has become less tolerant and respectful, while in relation to other matters such disputation has been suppressed by what is sometimes termed 'political correctness'. If we were writing our Constitution with a *tabula rasa*, I doubt that God would get a run, and not just because there are fewer believers and fewer Jews and Christians in modern Australia. I suspect the arguments of founding fathers like Barton, Higgins and O'Connor would find more favour with the electorate at large and with their fellow delegates. But given that we are not starting with a *tabula rasa*, respect for history, diversity and civility might continue to carry the day, maintaining the brief acknowledgement of the nation's reliance on blessing first commended to delegates by Patrick McMahon Glynn.

We would do well to heed Dyson Heydon's warning that even the law itself might be invoked by the elites to threaten religious institutions in the future. Especially in the new world of social media, we need to consider Heydon's warning that "some members of modern elites" could prevent public expression of religious thought "through ridicule and bullying" causing religion "to wither away even in the private sphere." But it may be an overstatement to claim that "what can have no public expression will eventually cease to have any private existence." And public expression does not necessarily entail explicit constitutional recognition. Ridicule and bullying have always been part of the armoury employed in the Australian public square by those populists (whether elitist or not) antipathetic to others who are unashamedly and committedly different, whether because of their culture, religion or political belief. Religious belief will always be contested space in constitutional discourse regardless of the religious convictions or entrenched atheism of elites. The challenge is to make that space civil and respectful. In this, our constitutional forefathers like Glynn, Barton, Higgins and O'Connor were exemplary. The nation is always the richer when leaders of their ilk step forward, despite their robust differences.

2

THE DEMAND FOR UNCONDITIONAL SURRENDER

Anne Henderson

"Modern elites do not demand tolerance. They demand unconditional surrender." In these two short sentences, Dyson Heydon captures the cancer of our modern Western times.

We have reached a point in our Western history where, to quote the vernacular of Australia's Henry Lawson, there is "higher education for the toilin' starvin' clown, An' the rich an' educated shall be educated down". Today, however, a somewhat different meaning can be attached to Lawson's words. For today, it seems, rich, poor, or somewhere in the middle, many fashionable voices of protest show scant regard for rational discussion, preferring a barracking roar in the face of any disagreement.

In a recent article for *The Times* of London, Hugo Rifkind summed up what he sees as a lazy politics where emotional name-calling has replaced any sort of rational debate. As he put it, "In Haringey, where I live, a mundane debate over how to fund a new generation of housing has become a bitter, emotional argument in which the word 'gentrification' is spat with all the venom of 'ethnic cleansing'."

Debate all too often in our age is being replaced by emotional overblown name-calling—"How many times," asks Rifkind, "have supporters of one sort of trade deal over another been described as 'treasonous' or 'traitors' or 'enemies of Britain'?" In conclusion, Rifkind sees a nasty and ill-educated outcome: "To bundle up policies with values and identities is to remove the possibility of honest debate, because your first principle becomes that the other side is undeserving of the courtesy of being listened to. Are we really going to pretend this is only happening in universities?"

As if to prove Rifkind's point, across half the globe, just as his piece was being published, the ABC's *Q&A* audience—well-known for its intolerance and Green/Left persuasion—that Monday night in Sydney was being cautioned by its not often so tightly reined presenter Tony Jones.

Neil McMahon, writing in the *Canberra Times*, reported the following day that "as the audience emitted a cross between a moan and a mild jeer [in response to Australian Chamber of Commerce and Industry CEO James Pearson] Jones cracked the whip with a smile: 'OK, we've got a long time to talk about this. Audience, you're going to hear a few things you don't agree with from time to time. Stay cool.'"

This same "moan" or "jeer", as Dyson Heydon rightly argues, has in recent decades become hostile to the organised religion of Christians and Jews. For the West, this is the great secular era. But it is a very particular secularism; a secularism that condemns the prominent religions of Western civilisation while sanctioning the rise of Islamic cultural norms, the prudery and intolerance of which fly in the face of Western social customs.

What began in Europe in the 1970s has spread across all democracies as the voices of the intellectual elites sing out—on public media and social media alike. At the heart of this selective secularism is Hollywood, with its tantalising images and stories that have spread a gospel of narcissism and materialism, all the while claiming a higher morality as its celebrants go about virtue-signalling on the fashionable issues of the day.

When Nancy Mitford, in her *Encounter* essay, "The English Aristocracy", took up British linguist Alan Ross's theory on the snobbery and separation of upper and lower classes through language as "U and Non-U", there was reasoned discussion and much laughter along the way. There is no such discussion or laughter in any attempt today to call out the rabid voices on climate change, coal, refugees, gay marriage, female empowerment, identity politics, gender fluidity or animal rights.

As a devout Catholic, Patrick McMahon Glynn knew both in his native Ireland and in Australia that the world could be harsh and testing. In spite of his education in the law at Middle Temple in London, being called to the Irish Bar in April 1879 and attending Trinity College Dublin, Glynn spent his first years as an immigrant Down Under scraping a living until he found success in a lawyer's practice at Kapunda, a mining town just north of Adelaide.

For all that, and in spite of much sectarianism dividing faiths and cultures at the time, Glynn was able to advance himself into politics on the back of his oratory and debater's skill. He belonged to an era where the political fight was nuanced, with the most persuasive arguments and personalities deciding the winner. Prevailing opinion there was and prejudice, to be sure, but spin, blind intolerance and violence to shut down debate was not the way of public discourse.

Glynn belonged to a society where belief in Christianity was the faith of a majority—in spite of the secular strains in the Australian colonial ethos. Heydon reminds us that "Glynn is traditionally assigned the authorship of that reference [in the Australian Constitution] to humble reliance on the blessing of Almighty God", and this despite opposition from atheists and secularists and Protestants in their different ways.

This may have been a sectarian world, where the secular, Catholic and Protestant divide was strongly recognised in the community. Yet, quite the opposite could happen—an outsider Irish Catholic Australian would triumph over the mainstream majority in a civilised dialogue.

Glynn's world was not an easy path for the outsider. Yet, it was a world that valued argument and persuasion front on. It was led by men who related to the actual community they represented. They communicated directly to their constituents.

Today, we stand before a new order where the leaders of reform and government must handle the consequences of "virtual" communication, via technology, that allows maverick challenges and virtual mob reaction to discourse. This is not only the fate of civic leaders—businesses and retail outlets, even movie makers, can find themselves under attack from media-driven campaigns.

In February 2018, Sony Pictures felt a need to issue a public apology over a scene in a new movie adapted from Beatrix Potter's *Peter Rabbit*. This followed calls for the movie to be withdrawn from cinemas because of a scene where Peter Rabbit and his furry friends pelt a man with blackberries he is allegic to. But he is an allergic man who is big, angry, and possessing intelligence superior enough to threaten the furry friends who have raided his garden.

The protest from Allergy UK collected 3,000 signatures online in three hours to a petition that claimed the scene "mocks the seriousness of allergic disease and is heartbreakingly disrespectful to the families of those who have lost loved ones to anaphylaxis". Groups followed up calling for a boycott of the film which expected to earn US$25 million in its opening weekend in the United States.

One might say that this is just the market of ideas and all is fair in love and war. Yet, such virtual (and virtue) protesting with attempts to shut down freedom of speech and association often turns ugly. Two recent examples alone testify to the damning nature of groupthink intolerance.

At James Cook University, Professor Peter Ridd is no climate change sceptic. He is as green as it gets. However, he has taken on the university over claims that the Great Barrier Reef has suffered irreparable damage. His findings conflict with the official teaching on the reef at James Cook University. Ridd is a lecturer and researcher in physics and marine geophysics, with more than 100 peer-reviewed articles to his name, who has undertaken extensive research on coral reefs. He has worked at James Cook University since 1989.

In February 2018, Peter Ridd was given a 'Final Censure' from the university because of his criticism of the process by which the university's science faculties have reached their official version of marine life on the Great Barrier Reef. In May, the university sacked Ridd for failing to comply with James Cook University's code of conduct alleging the "disrespect he showed for the university as a senior employee".

Ridd has demonstrated that the reef is capable of renewal and has renewed itself often but this does not fit the official James Cook University belief. Said Ridd: "The science is coming out not properly checked, tested or replicated and this is a great shame because we really need to be able to trust our scientific institutions."

Ridd is fighting the case and has commenced proceedings in the Federal Court to assert his academic freedom to discuss scientific integrity. For all that, the case has many mediaeval overtones—as with

Galileo and Rome, science has been overtaken by censorship. Where Galileo was found to have to have contradicted holy scripture, Ridd has contradicted the official teaching of James Cook University.

Then we have the shrill activism from marriage equality supporters in 2017. During Australia's debate over same-sex marriage, its supporters took on figures with connections to Christian churches. Ironically, though, not figures in Muslim churches where same-sex marriage is far more aggressively opposed.

In March 2017, IBM was targeted by militant gay rights advocates who condemned the company because one of its executives was linked to a Christian organisation. No matter that IBM as a company had come out as a marriage equality advocate. It was not enough. Gay rights activists insisted that the fact that IBM managing partner Mark Allaby was on the board of Lachlan Macquarie Institute, which runs an internship program for young Christians, was incompatible with IBM's public support for marriage equality. Shortly after the attack, Allaby resigned from his board position at Lachlan Macquarie Institute. Allaby had earlier been pressured to stand down from the board of the Australian Christian Lobby when he held a position at PricewaterhouseCoopers which like IBM was a supporter of marriage equality.

The Western world's dilemmas over ethics and moral boundaries have come as the decline in religion has hastened. In the early days of Australian colonial settlement, Governor Macquarie appointed clergymen to every district in the new colony and commanded that convicts attend Sunday services. He believed that Christian principles would ensure that coming generations would be "dutiful and obedient to their parents and superiors" and that such guidance would make them "honest, faithful and useful members of society". That God was included in the founding fathers' Constitution supports the view that religion was still considered paramount in a majority of Australian lives decades later.

Today, however, while Christian practices have long permeated Australia's legal tradition, it is hard not to feel that a growing lack of any religion, in a majority, and a broadening of the variety of faiths on offer means that these traditions are under challenge. As Augusto

Zimmermann argues in his paper in Volume 5 of the *Western Australian Jurist*, the Governor-General "swears allegiance to the Queen under section 42 of the Constitution, binding himself [herself] to the principles expressed in the Queen's oaths of office. These oaths include significant Christian undertakings." To what extent these facts are merely symbolic, in relation to how Australia thinks and conducts its business in the twenty-first century, is now debatable.

It is not only Australia's mainstream Christian institutions that are witnessing a falling away of belief. Institutional authority itself is under attack. Online targeting of businesses and organisations by maverick rights activists is a regular phenomenon. The age of the internet has given individuals more power to disrupt—so much so that 'disruptive technology' is now a buzzword and a lucrative business opportunity.

In a world where minority rights have taken over in the virtue-signalling of the media and middle-class elites, alienation among pluralist societies in the West is a given. Where once anti-Americanism was the preserve of the far left, today it permeates the groupthink of the educated and ordinary. Western self-hatred is not uncommon.

Even as Western society comes under attack from Islamist terrorists, a left-leaning American president can find it hard to tag such terrorists as 'Islamic'. The increasing numbers of minority Islamic communities (and hence of voters) in Western countries has made political leaders wary of giving offence. And this to such an extent that media presenters and public figures tiptoe around calling out repressive Islamic law and customs—such as discrimination against women and gays—for fear of offence. Imagine what an ABC presenter such as Julia Baird might do with any Anglican archbishop who recommended disciplining Christian wives by 'not hard' beatings.

The left-leaning conversion of universities over recent decades has created a class of professionals and voters—most of whom, in Australia, are fans of the ABC—that pushes back instinctively on issues such as the State of Israel, American hegemony, climate change scepticism, nuclear energy, coal, the Liberal and National parties, church-based education and so on. Largely, this is the same collective that cries out against Christianity and Judaism.

But to what extent the attack on specific churches is an attack on faith and believers as such is hard to fathom. It is, in many instances, more a pushback against older models of institutional order and authority. Where Christianity once formed the basis of civil order, it is now under attack in an age of new norms, beliefs and rampant individual conscience. In this, ironically, Catholicism has been mixed in with what used to be its rival Christian churches in the days of sectarian divides that began with Martin Luther. At the 500th anniversary of Martin Luther's 95 Theses, Catholic and Protestant alike acknowledged the significance of that date. And both recognised the lessons to be learned from the centuries of sectarian bloodletting that followed, on both sides.

It is an understatement to say that Christian churches are relatively empty at regular services these days. In the urban outer suburbs, there are still lively communities that gather around Catholic and evangelical church centres. But these are mostly supported by the schools, community services and camaraderie they provide. Births, marriages and deaths, along with schools, are now the mainstay of Catholic parishes and churches.

However, while there are stiff challenges around setting a creed and strict guidelines, for any church that preaches to highly educated Western flocks, it is a challenge church leaders and communities should be able to meet. The state may have taken over many of the services that were once left for churches and faith groups to deliver but, across the virtual world that humans have now created, there is still a hunger for community, caring and intellectual guidance in sound living which the Judeo-Christian tradition can sate.

Dyson Heydon reminds us that the freedoms enjoyed by the West have been made possible by Judeo-Christian principles. The principles of argument, of redefinition of the sacred texts, the refining of teaching and a movement—however cautious—with the times. As Dyson Heydon argues: "Even the great Councils of the fourth and fifth centuries prefigured the modern liberal world, as they tried to thrash out fundamental questions in long debates, like a nineteenth-century representative legislature."

In public, P. M. Glynn was never embarrassed to speak out when religious issues arose. His speech to the House of Representatives in 1910 (on the death of King Edward VII) over removing words offensive to Catholics from an address to the Crown on the coronation oath was described by the Melbourne *Age* as "a brilliant piece of cultured oratory".

Glynn argued in that speech that:

> The spirit of intolerance which once, perhaps in varying degrees, was displayed by mistaken zealots of every creed, is not the spirit of our days . . . [The terms of the oath] are out of keeping with the finer spirit of this age, and really unworthy of a people whose character, on the whole, is, I believe, as frank and generous as their love of justice is proverbial and inspiring.

The motion to remove words offensive to Catholics was carried by the House of Representatives.

Yet, Glynn experienced quite a few challenges to his faith in Christianity. As a bachelor in Kapunda in the late nineteenth century, he began to question the exclusivity of Christianity and its belief in "one true God". He abhorred the materialism of some in the Protestant faith. Even at one point writing to his brother James that "Church of Englandism is not Christianity at all". In the same letter, Glynn's characteristic quick wit and sense of irony noted that an Anglican bishop in Melbourne—Dr Fraser—had "died leaving £85,000 at his bankers, not a bad sum . . . to get for dinning into his flock's ears that it is more difficult for a rich man to get to Heaven etc."

Glynn's enduring sense of his faith eventually resolved itself in what he called "the dreams of our childhood". And this he defined, writing: "At all events, we cannot do better than really follow, to the best of our capacities, the essential teachings of Jesus of Nazareth".

In the spirit of P. M. Glynn, then, what better vision could there be for those who would continue the spirit and practice of Australia's Judeo-Christian traditions. The way forward is, as P. M. Glynn would have had it, argument, informed conscience and the courage to promote intelligent discourse.

3

THE FAILURE OF CONTEMPORARY POLITICAL DEBATE

Paul Kelly

Religious freedom was the missing element in the long debate in Australia leading to the legalising of same-sex marriage in late 2017. This was a failure of policy and parliamentary responsibility. Whether it will be corrected following the report of the Ruddock committee to the Turnbull government in May 2018 remains to be seen. But the response of the government and parliament following this report on religious freedom will become a benchmark for our society and its values.

Amid the gloom of 2017 on the religious freedom front there was a rare shining light—the inaugural Glynn Lecture by former High Court judge, Dyson Heydon. In a lecture of historical range and lethal precision, Heydon identified the weakness of legal provisions in Australia for religious liberty. Some critics seek to ensure religious freedom remains inferior to other rights in our law. Others are more ambitious—their objective is to marginalise or silence Christianity in a project that rejects "a large part of the entire life and history of the nation."

In my view the main contribution of the Glynn Lecture was to put the religious freedom contest onto the philosophical, historical and cultural plane where it belongs. Sadly, it has been treated as an afterthought in the same-sex marriage debate by a majority in the parliament and the media. The intellectual poverty of this debate and its campaign against free expression were extraordinary.

The purpose of this essay is to review aspects of the same-sex marriage debate and the postal plebiscite that finally led to its resolution. This offers a background perspective to many of the arguments advanced by Dyson Heydon.

In December 2017 the parliament legislated same-sex marriage amid jubilation. Yet this occurred in a deeply divided parliament, a reality largely unreported, where every effort to bolster individual and religious freedom was crushed. The final vote, carried with only four lonely dissidents, provoked embraces, tears, flag-waving and cheering from the public galleries amid cries that "love has won", leading to the impression that the parliament had come together. In fact, the reverse was the case.

This was a winner-takes-all result. The majority prevailed and the minority was vanquished. The ramifications will last for many years. The contest, with its inevitable result, was waged on the floor of the House of Representatives throughout Thursday 7 December. In effect, it constituted the arrival of the new Australia and the demise of the old. The debate left no doubt what this means: the new Australia enshrines the principle of non-discrimination to guarantee diversity and will accord this priority over the principle of religious freedom, goodwill for which is eroding within progressive politics.

Bill Shorten declared it was a "time for healing". Malcolm Turnbull said it was a triumph for love, equality and unity. The sense of personal liberation at the conclusion was euphoric and emotional. During the day, however, the story was different—there was just a punishing series of votes in which a majority of Coalition MPs were repudiated in their efforts to secure same-sex marriage with religious freedom protections.

For Turnbull, it was a singular win and writes him into the pages of history—he delivered the plebiscite and legislated before Christmas, as he had pledged. Within sections of the Coalition there is sheer relief that same-sex marriage is legislated and off the agenda, which means they won't need to discuss it any more. Contrary to impressions, however, there is no internal settlement, no uniting of the whole nation. Turnbull delivered same-sex marriage but failed to deliver the religious freedom protections he espoused. This was inevitable because the numbers did not exist for them. Will the numbers re-emerge for them next year or the year after?

The Prime Minister never once during the day rose to his feet to defend these enshrined principles, while still voting for three of the many religious freedoms amendments. For a majority of Coalition ministers and MPs, same-sex marriage is established on legislative foundations that give them grave concern.

Turnbull presided but Labor and the Liberal progressives dictated the terms. The Liberal Party engaged in a brave debate based on conscience, which heard member speaking against member. The conservatives tried to secure changes to safeguard charities against discrimination, to guarantee parental rights over marriage values their children are taught, to protect conscience for civil marriage celebrants and military marriage celebrants, to protect individuals when expressing a view about marriage and against being discriminated against for their beliefs, and to build into our laws religious freedom principles from the International Covenant on Civil and Political Rights. Each was defeated.

Each defeat was met with applause from the public galleries filled for the day-long debate with supporters of the same-sex marriage cause. Parliament was not just embracing a new freedom in same-sex marriage; the bell was tolling for protection of religious belief. Many politicians will deny this. But these are hollow words, given their votes and their speeches. Devoid of a satisfactory settlement, Australia's culture war will continue. Its intensity and timing now depends on how the radical activists pursue their continuing campaign to erode further religious principles, norms and institutions.

Throughout the day the Labor Party voted as a bloc. Its discipline held on every vote. No Labor member broke ranks; few uttered a sentence of meaningful support for religious freedom. Labor said all the amendments were unnecessary or dangerous, or both. It refused to admit the slightest threat to religious freedom in Australia despite considerable evidence to the contrary. For Labor, the issue of religious freedom is a party issue and that will not change. The long struggle over same-sex marriage has witnessed a historic shift in the values, culture and character of Labor. The critical question for Labor is whether, now same-sex marriage has been legislated, it can adopt a more balanced perspective and address the legal loopholes around religious freedom.

This event was one of the greatest defeats for conservatives in many decades. It was predictable since the conservatives had long mismanaged this issue and the Turnbull government, in a position of weakness, was unable to spell out religious freedoms and protections at the start of the postal plebiscite process. The challenge for the Liberal Party arising from the Ruddock review (headed by former Immigration Minister and Attorney-General, Philip Ruddock) is existential: how serious is the Liberal Party's belief in religious freedom? This will be an important moment for the future of conservative politics in this country. The consequences would be severe if the Coalition government is seen to walk away from the idea of religious freedom or to pretend there was no problem.

Labor had a valid argument during last year's debate saying the issue of religious freedom should be postponed to the Ruddock report. Labor was fixated on securing the same-sex marriage bill without amendment and nothing was to be allowed to hold up this imperative. The claims made by Labor and the bill's advocate during the debate were correct—that the religious freedom issue was not part of the postal plebiscite. It was not voted on at that time. This served as a significant argument for voting in favour of same-sex marriage and voting down the amendments.

The fate of the main amendments was as follows: Andrew Hastie's proposal to protect free speech and guarantee parents' rights was defeated 87-55; Scott Morrison's amendment to protect charities and prevent them being stripped of funding for their beliefs was lost 82-59; Alex Hawke's amendment to protect rights for military celebrants was defeated 87-59; Andrew Broad's two proposals to protect charities and faith-based bodies were lost 86-52 and 85-60; proposals from Michael Sukkar to extend the new definition of marriage to also include 'man-woman' marriage and protect conscience for civil celebrants was defeated 97-43; and Sarah Henderson, a supporter of same-sex marriage, proposed amendments essentially to incorporate into law the religious freedom declarations from article 18 of the International Covenant on Civil and Political Rights, and was defeated 79-63, the closest that cause came to victory.

Turnbull voted for the Henderson, Hawke and Broad amendments (the Broad amendment relating to faith-based charities). These were substantial efforts to secure religious freedom. Turnbull abstained from the other votes. But the Prime Minister should have spoken. In the end, only two cabinet ministers, Morrison and Barnaby Joyce, spoke to the amendments. Morrison and Peter Dutton, as Liberal cabinet ministers, voted for all the amendments. But a cabinet majority and a Coalition party room majority was conspicuous in most of the lost religious freedom votes. In short, there was no dispute about where the majority of government MPs lined up—and no dispute about their defeat. A small but influential group of Liberal progressives opposed most of the religious freedom proposals.

The reasons for Labor's opposition were best articulated by its legal affairs spokesman Mark Dreyfus and assistant spokeswoman Terri Butler. They tended to fall under several headings—that some of the proposals were genuinely radical in nature; were unacceptable because they would wind back anti-discrimination laws; required much more elaborate assessment and should await the Ruddock review; addressed problems that did not exist because there was no danger to religious freedom; involved cherry-picking religious rights without full consideration of other rights; that Dean Smith's private member's bill on same-sex marriage was not the proper vehicle for many of these broad-based amendments; and that the immediate priority was passage of the bill without delay.

Many of these were substantial arguments. They reflected the near-impossible situation facing the conservatives, who knew they must try to exert leverage before the bill passed, since after it passed they would have virtually none. In the end, their efforts were doomed and everyone moving amendments knew that. They were smashed on the numbers.

What might be different during any future debate is that any vote on the Ruddock report's recommendations is likely to be a vote on a government bill, not a private member's bill—whether that makes a decisive difference remains to be seen. In speaking to the amendments Tony Abbott laid down a serious charge: "The problem that this House is wrestling with today is the absence of detailed consideration of freedom of speech, of conscience and of religion, which both the Prime Minister and the Leader of the Opposition promised would be given to us before the bill was finalised. A promise was made by the leaders of this Parliament and the promise has not adequately been delivered upon."

During the debate on the amendments Morrison warned: "There is a clear demand for this. I fear what other members have said—that we will have to revisit this issue once the injury has happened. We could take steps now to prevent that injury. I, like other members of the government, am disappointed that the Labor Party have decided not to have a fair dinkum conscience vote on these amendments at all."

The Attorney-General, George Brandis, was correct when he said the successful bill and the event was "not owned by the Liberal Party or the Labor Party or any political party" but by the people who had voted 'yes'. The pivotal event leading to the legislation was the postal plebiscite result that recorded a 'yes' vote at 61.6 per cent and a 'no' vote of 38.4 per cent. There is no question the parliamentary vote reflected majority public opinion. A Newspoll, however, published in September showed that 57 per cent wanted same-sex marriage as the law and an even bigger 62 per cent wanted religious freedoms protected. The legislated result honoured the first sentiment and dishonoured the second.

A notable feature of the plebiscite campaign had been the refusal of the Yes camp to concede any legitimacy to warnings of the No camp about the risks to religious freedom and belief. The Yes camp was resolute: it said such warnings were an unjustified scare and an egregious tactic without substance. At the same time the Yes camp had nothing to say about the actual argument—it simply refused to engage. A different response from the Yes camp would have been to say: "OK, let's legislate on the basis of religious freedom protections." But such a concession was never in prospect. However, during the campaign Turnbull felt obliged to remark he believed in religious freedom "more strongly" than in same-sex marriage. It is something he should be expected to honour.

The remark is significant because it contradicts the assumption on which the debate has been conducted for many years, namely that same-sex marriage is more important than religious freedom. Among the litany of private members' bills proposed in federal parliament in recent years, none ever attempted to address religious freedom issues for individuals and institutions. There was no rhetoric to this effect, no debate, no pressure. Same-sex marriage advocates in government and parliament assumed that, apart from protections surrounding the wedding ceremony, no wider protections were needed.

At the same time, however, a range of constitutional experts have evaluated the protections for religious freedom in Australia and found them to be wanting. This was documented most recently in the submissions to the Senate Select Committee on the draft Brandis bill on same-sex marriage and in the committee's February 2017 report. The Brandis draft had no standing and no cabinet authorisation. It was, however, influential and Dean Smith's bill that became the model for the parliamentary debate was similar to the Brandis draft.

Chairman of the Senate committee, South Australian Liberal David Fawcett, said in his foreword to the report: "If Australia is to remain a plural, tolerant society where different views are valued and legal, legislators must recognise that this change will require careful, simultaneous consideration of a wide range of specialist areas of law as opposed to the common perception that it involves just a few words in one act of parliament." The core question raised by the report was whether individuals, institutions, churches, schools, charitable organisations and businesses would be protected if they held to the traditional view of marriage after same-sex marriage was law. The Senate committee report showed they would not and, as already outlined, the issue was not corrected by the government in the final bill.

The committee after reviewing the landscape said: "Overall the evidence supports the need for current protections for religious freedom to be enhanced. This would most appropriately be achieved through the inclusion of 'religious belief' in federal anti-discrimination law." Interestingly, this was the view of the whole committee. Many bodies supported this recommendation in their submissions. Human Rights

Commissioner Ed Santow observed: "You could have a standalone statute that specifically dealt with freedom of religion or you could expand the Racial Discrimination Act."

University of Sydney law professor Patrick Parkinson welcomed protections for ministers of religion and for marriage celebrants of the kind found in the Smith Bill but said this was far from sufficient. "In certain sections of the community, there is now deep hatred expressed for people of faith," Parkinson said. "Provisions are required to protect people from discrimination on account of whatever views they may hold about marriage, whether they are opposed to same-sex marriage or in favour of it." He said it must be made lawful for any person or entity to express an opinion that accords with a religious or conscientious belief about marriage. He advocated laws to protect people or entities in relation to employment, contracting, academic, trade or professional qualification, accommodation, education and administration of Commonwealth laws and programs.

Institute for Civil Society executive director Mark Sneddon summarised his views based on his submission to the Senate committee: "I am extremely concerned about the lack of legal protection across this country in terms of freedom of conscience, belief and religion for people who support traditional marriage. These protections are far less than those for people who support same-sex marriage. Yet it is those who support traditional marriage who are more susceptible to actions . . . from government bodies and commercial organisations. Where persons hold the traditional view of marriage not on grounds of religious belief, they have no protection under federal, state and territory anti-discrimination laws or the Fair Work Act. If they hold the traditional view of marriage on the grounds of religious belief they have no protection under federal anti-discrimination law, no protection under NSW or South Australian anti-discrimination laws and some protection under the anti-discrimination laws of the other states or territories but only for individuals and not organisations."

The Senate committee was provided with examples of prejudicial treatment of people and institutions because they supported traditional marriage. Dean Smith was correct to argue his bill had more protections than anything likely to come from a Labor government. But this could not gainsay its omissions.

Australia is not going to be transformed by having a few hundred or a few thousand gays getting married. But it is going to be transformed by legalising same-sex marriage in a framework where religious protections are weak and where the ongoing campaign for gay rights and transformed norms in our society is designed to further weaken individual liberty and the related freedom of religion, some of the most vital freedoms we possess. This is a longstanding objective of the Greens. It is the position of wide sections of the ALP left. It is an ideological aspiration of much of the progressive class in this country and in the West.

In this context the Glynn Lecture by Dyson Heydon is a text for our times.

4

REASONS TO FEAR WAR

M. A. Casey

Wars have a way of spreading. Sometimes this is because of unintended or unforeseen consequences. Sometimes it is because of the peculiar form of logic which takes hold to rule out turning back, to exclude other possibilities from consideration, and to funnel everything into one bitter, ineluctable course, where the only way out is through. Wars of ideology, whether actual or metaphorical, are particularly prone to this danger, and all the more relentless and unreasoning because of it.

What Dyson Heydon calls "the current war on religious faith" is an example. It is no localised conflict, despite some official accounts which represent it as being strictly limited to the elimination of discrimination. As Heydon points out, it is war prosecuted less by legal means (at this stage) than by "ridicule and bullying", seeking to exclude the expression of religious claims in public discussion and to confine it to the private sphere. There it is meant to wither away quietly, because "what can have no public expression will eventually cease to have any private expression". While "section 116 of the Constitution prevents the enactment of any Commonwealth law prohibiting the free exercise of religion", continual "vilification, insults, derision, scorn, fake outrage and bullying mockery . . . can do as much to prevent the free exercise of religion as any law falling foul of section 116".

Heydon argues that "even those who are not members of religious institutions and have no particular sympathy for them" should fear this war, because it is likely to extend to other areas. There is an inevitability to this because of the priority given to autonomy by the elites Heydon discusses, not just over religiosity but over other forms of solidarity and sociability as well. Two of its most prominent manifestations at the moment are sexuality and identity. As these examples show, the focus on autonomy often gives rise to some critical questions about respect for the dignity of each person, individual freedom, fairness and discrimination, which need to be addressed. The problem arises not only from the particular scope and definition given to these issues, or the way in which they are pursued. The much more important question is whether autonomy, especially when it is prioritised over solidarity and the common good, is a durable basis for a just and decent society, which itself depends on holding people together and not making them strangers to each other.

Heydon's point about the likelihood of the war on faith spreading to other areas can be thrown into sharper relief by considering some remarks made by the Hungarian Prime Minister, Viktor Orbán, in a speech he gave to university students in July 2018. In this speech, Orbán listed five principles for the development of central Europe as he sees it. Three of them are of interest for present purposes. Firstly, Orbán proposed "that every European country has the right to defend its Christian culture, and to reject the ideology of multiculturalism". Another principle was that "every country has the right to defend the traditional family model, and is entitled to assert that every child has the right to a mother and father". The third principle of interest was "that every country has the right to defend its borders, and it has the right to reject immigration".[1] None of these propositions is un-sayable in Australia today, but for the elites with whom Heydon is concerned, the saying of them is more than sufficient to cast doubt on the decency and humanity of those who say them. For these elites, each proposition, in one way or another, is discriminatory, exclusionary, and at least implicitly phobic towards different categories of people. That a figure such as Orbán should propose such principles as the basis of national policy and regional co-operation serves as decisive proof that they are beyond the pale.

Leave to one side the merits or otherwise of these propositions, the motivations of particular politicians in putting them forward, and what they may or may not entail in terms of practical policy. The critical point of interest is the suspicion and hostility with which their mere utterance is treated at the commanding heights of politics and culture in societies like our own. Orbán's approach to democracy has given rise to concern for many serious reasons, reminding us that is not only autonomy which can be prioritised over solidarity and the common good. He has also caused consternation with his concept of "illiberal democracy", a phrase which depends for its resonance on the problematic nature of what have become some of the defining moral commitments of liberal democracy. These include the repudiation of the Christian heritage of Western societies, the valourisation of newer forms of sexuality, marriage and family life over traditional understandings, and the free movement of people and capital through more or less open borders; and a mode of enforcing these commitments which includes "vilification, insults, derision, scorn, fake outrage and bullying mockery".

The war of derision Heydon describes is not only directed against faith or ideas usually associated with conservatism. It is also being prosecuted in other, very different climes. Feminists who reject the transgender push are attacked for being phobes and haters, and those who express concern about the fallout from the MeToo movement are treated as brainwashed at best and traitors at worst.[2] In the wake of the 2016 American presidential election, the impeccably liberal thinker Mark Lilla argued that American liberalism needed to focus more on what united people than on identity politics. For this, he was likened by an academic colleague to a Ku Klux Klan leader and accused of "making white supremacy respectable again".[3] A whole range of ideas and perspectives across political lines are now susceptible to being characterised as forms of hate speech which "denigrate" and therefore "inflict serious harm" on "marginalised groups". The logic of this is that vulnerable people must be protected from debates and discussions which may cause them offence or hurt—which means that such debates and discussions should not be allowed.[4]

A better appreciation of the history and lived experience of different marginalised groups has helped to further humanise democratic societies and to deepen tolerance in the true sense of the word. The politics associated with it, however, which is itself a working-out of liberal democracy's underlying commitment to radical autonomy, "prioritizes the emotional world of the inner self over the rational examination of issues in the outside world and privileges sincerely held opinions over a process of reasoned deliberation". The result is that any statement or fact taken by someone to be "offensive" to their "sense of self-worth is often seen as grounds for silencing or disparaging the individual who made it".[5] Heydon observes that "there is more wrong with the approach of the elites than discourtesy". The readiness to shut down discussions and to shut out facts by saying "that's offensive" suggests not only an unwillingness, but more significantly an inability, to present a point of view and to argue for it with those who are unpersuaded or who disagree. As Heydon reminds us, "to shout is not to argue. To censor is not to reason. To bawl is not to engage in persuasion".

To say, as Francis Fukuyama has commented, that "the preoccupation with identity has clashed with the need for civic discourse", is to put the matter very mildly.[6] Claire Fox places the repudiation of free speech at the centre of "illiberal liberalism", which runs the risk of becoming "the PC midwife to authoritarianism".[7] Fox comes from a very different perspective to that of Viktor Orbán, but her observation sheds light on Orbán's populist idea of illiberal democracy. Some see this phrase as the boast of incipient dictatorship, which does not really help in understanding the particular political appeal it encapsulates. If it is understanding that we are seeking, it may be better read as a rejection of the idea that democracy is synonymous with a form of liberalism that has lost its bearings and increasingly shows itself willing to descend into madness.

Free speech—like freedom of religion—used to be considered one of the pre-eminent markers of a democratic society, and as Heydon points out (referencing Peter Kurti), "traditionally liberalism aimed to protect individuals against the encoaching power of the state". Today it is a more advanced idea of liberalism (or liberal democracy) rather than the state which is most likely to encroach on rights such as freedom of speech and religion and the lives of individuals, deploying semi-soft means of intimidation and harassment such as political correctness, speech codes, safe spaces, no platforming and social media hate campaigns.

Not so much in Australia, but certainly overseas, these means have even extended to loss of employment and the refusal or cancellation of accreditation to study, teach or practice a profession. Sometimes this involves the instrumentalities of the state, most obviously when it comes to protracted and expensive judicial or administrative processes, which work very effectively in signalling to the general public what is expected. Even in this case, however, the initiative usually arises from society itself, from individuals and groups, rather than from government departments, highlighting a peculiar characterisic of this situation: the spontaneous citizen-enforcement of liberal democracy's moral commitments by institutions and non-government organisations, businesses and employers, community and activist groups, and individuals in public and private settings who are offended by something said or written.

Reflecting on the situation in Europe in 2017, the distinguished authors of the Paris Statement described freedom of speech as "freedom of conscience made manifest". Our deepest beliefs compel us to speak as well as act, and this freedom must be protected if the voice of conscience is to be heard. The signatories to this statement are not "free speech absolutists", a term used to characterise and discredit defenders of free speech as extremists. To the extent that it is useful at all, this term might more aptly be applied to those in the decades of the late twentieth century who worked so effectively to make obscenity a form of free "speech". Sociologically, this should be seen as an important milestone, not only for the way it contributed to the corrosion of trust and friendship and the increase in isolation and loneliness in the culture more generally, but also for the parasitic incoherence it planted in the concept of freedom of speech, which is now turning against its host and free speech properly understood. There are now few effective controls on obscenity, despite its disastrous personal and social consequences, but increasing restrictions on what can be said about political or social issues, despite its disastrous consequences for politics and our sense of a life in common. Many of these restrictions are spontaneously enforced through what is in effect a form of denunciation. "Recourse to denunciation is a sign of the decadence of our present moment", the authors of the Paris Statement observe. "Language is a delicate instrument, and it is debased when used as a bludgeon". "Verbal intimidation" must be rejected in favour of a renewed commitment to protecting "those who speak reasonably, even if we think their views mistaken". Liberalism "in the best sense" means "robust public debate free from all threats of violence and coercion".[8]

Freedom of speech faces these various pressures despite being almost synonymous with democracy and readily understood as a fundamental human right by almost everyone. Freedom of religion has neither of these advantages in Australia. Heydon describes how the elites, "in seeking to marginalise and silence Christianity, are not only rejecting the cultural tradition of Christianity" but "a large part of the entire life and history of the nation", which is also both "the source of the modern world and of their own favoured position within it". Beyond these elites, however, most Australians would have only a vague idea at best of the important contribution made to the Australian achievement by religion in general and Christianity in particular. It is a fundamental proposition of Australian life that all human beings are equal, and this equality in turn is the basis of the enormous individual freedom we enjoy. Elites and the general population value these propositions highly, but are complacent about both their foundations and the part these foundations play in ensuring a continuing commitment to equality and freedom in our country. As Heydon emphasises (citing Larry Siedentop), we have forgotten that it is "natural inequality, and the natural superiority of the few over the many," which is the default of the human condition, not the strange idea that all human beings were created equal.

Complacency and forgetfulness make it easier for the elites to be hostile to both religion and religious freedom. For the general population, however, the problem is less hostility than incomprehension and suspicion. The incomprehension is not difficult to understand. What religious freedom means, why it is important, and why it is a human right are questions that many people in Australia would be unclear about, and not just the 30 per cent or so in the 2016 census who indicated that they have no religion. For people who are not religious, it can take quite a leap of imagination and empathy to understand why it is so important to others. For people who profess or practise a religion, it is often very personal and local, and the larger public dimensions of religious belief can be remote from their everyday focus.

At its simplest, religious freedom is a form of basic fairness with four parts. It allows people to determine their own beliefs about the purpose and meaning of life, to organise their lives around these beliefs, and to put them into practice with other people who share them. It also protects people from being forced to act against their beliefs. These four elements locate religious freedom as part of a much larger whole with significant implications for many things beyond the life of faith, which also explains its importance. Religious freedom encompasses the dignity of the person; other rights such as freedom of thought, freedom of expression, freedom of association, and freedom of conscience; forms of social co-operation and service to the community; and habits and commitments which help to foster trust, resilience and openness in a good society. Religious freedom is a human right because rights protect the things that make it possible for people to flourish both as individuals and as members of communities, and this includes the powerful need we have to make sense of our existence. There are different ways, small and large, of doing this, and different ways of avoiding the problem too, but a significant and continuing part of the human story involves seeking out answers not of our own making, which are part of something greater than ourselves and greater than the world immediately around us. This requires freedom: to consider, reflect, debate, change our minds and to form beliefs and convictions. Human beings are creedal creatures. Religious freedom arises from and protects this aspect of our nature.

Suspicion towards religion is also not difficult to explain, especially in a context where corruption, abuse of power and trust, failing to protect those who are vulnerable, and covering up crimes have been brought to light in some religious institutions. There is also a more general and longer-standing wariness which makes not only religion but religious freedom suspect. Common examples are claims that religion produces conflict, that it is a way of imposing beliefs on other people, that it is at odds with the values of secular democratic society and probably a threat to them. This suspicion places religious freedom in a category all of its own: as a dangerous human right that needs to be kept closely in check.

There is no doubt that religion has been and continues to be a source of conflict. Violence and corruption make a mockery of the high vision of human purpose and destiny which different religions propose, and unsurprisingly this has a powerful effect in discrediting their claims. Conflict is one of the plagues of the human condition. We have proven ourselves capable of fighting over just about anything—land, resources, wealth, power, and perhaps most destructively of all, ideas. While it is quite rightly a source of particular dismay, it should really come as no surprise that we are willing to fight each other over religious questions too, and to use religion to justify other conflicts. Religious freedom, however, is intended to be a means of preventing conflict between people with different convictions, whether those convictions are religious or non-religious. It helps to create a society where, despite profound and even irreconcilable differences, people can learn how to live together as a community, and not just apart from each other in their own bubbles. This requires a willingness to respect differences in a spirit of friendship rather than hostility. It is a common lament across divides currently that we seem to have forgotten how to do this. Possibly some deeper reflection about religious freedom can help in its rediscovery.

There is no doubt too that history offers many examples of religion being used to impose values on people and punish or persecute those who do not conform. Religion does not have a monopoly on this tendency of course, nor is a strict secularist mindset any guarantee against it. In Victoria, the law requires doctors and other health professionals to facilitate access to abortion, even if they have conscientious objections to it, and in other countries there is strong pressure to prevent people from working in healthcare, or to exclude them from doing so, if they are not willing to help provide "the full range of services". It is important to be clear about whether the objection is to imposing values on other people as a matter of principle, or only a selective objection depending on the particular values being imposed.

Heydon highlights the relativism of the elites on this point: there is no in-principle objection to imposing values. Catholic teaching on religious freedom offers a better approach. One of its first principles is respect for freedom, and specifically the freedom of each individual to seek the truth and to shape their life in accordance with it. If it is to be genuine, faith, or for that matter any other form of conviction, must be freely chosen. Most people want this for themselves, and so we should be willing to allow it for others. It is strange that this has become so difficult to navigate. As our society becomes more sophisticated, more prosperous and more diverse, live and let live should become easier. Instead, the desire to impose values seems to grow stronger, and in Australia this is not primarily from religious sources. As Heydon remarks, "modern elites do not demand tolerance. They demand unconditional surrender. They want absolute victory for an uncontestable dogma which is unchallengeable".

Religious freedom is also important in clarifying the role of religion in a secular democracy, and more specifically the rights of individuals, communities, organisations and services motivated by the convictions of a religious faith. The separation of church and state is a critical safeguard for both. Government should be secular and for the good of all, but this does not mean that religious people lose their rights as citizens to contribute to debate and public policy and to bring religious perspectives to their own participation in politics. Religious communities are subject to the law and have to work within the same procedures and regulations that apply to everyone else, but this does not mean that a government can determine a faith community's beliefs and doctrines or how they are to be interpreted or practised. It is also important to be clear that religious freedom is not an absolute. Like other rights, it is limited by the duty to respect the common good and the rights and freedoms of others. When different claims are in tension with each other, we need to find a compromise and a way forward which respects the rights of all involved. The approach we take to this task matters enormously. Generosity and mutual respect are more productive than mistrust and enmity, especially when there is good faith on both sides. Remembering that human rights are meant to go together rather than pull apart is also essential if resolving differences is not to be reduced to a zero-sum game which calls the whole idea of human rights into question.

A significant part of our modern understanding of human rights is shaped by the great international agreements of the post-war era, especially the Universal Declaration of Human Rights and the International Covenant on Civil and Political Rights. It is interesting to wonder whether religious freedom would be included in these documents or given the same importance if they were to be written today. Among other factors, its inclusion in the Universal Declaration of Human Rights, written in the immediate aftermath of the Second World War, reflected not only the way religious freedom was targeted for destruction by dictatorships, but also the role it played in empowering people to resist and to call evil by its name. Religion can foster conformity, but it can also enable resistance to conformity. Systems of power hate it because it helps to keep courage and resilience alive in individuals, and a sense of solidarity and hope alive in communities. As a source of resistance, it helped to bring about the end of the slave trade in nineteenth-century Britain, the end of segregation in the United States in the 1960s, and the end of communism in Europe in 1989. In Australia today, it helps to ensure that we continue to have many voices refusing to be silent about the homeless and marginalised, about refugees, about the unborn and the disabled, about the sick and dying. Do we really have so many of these voices that we can do without those who speak from their religious convictions?

The elites' "tyranny of relativism" is a key focus of Heydon's Glynn Lecture. This tyranny "combines a relativist conception of truth with an absolutist moralism", but as the emergence of populist movements has shown, it is a game which can also be played by others. For all players, truth is not a matter of the strongest arguments but the strongest emotions.[9] You know the truth when you *feel* it. For a long time in the West it has been assumed that the absence of truth—a reality not of our making, greater than our individual perspectives, knowable but unbending before our will or emotions—is the condition of the most complete freedom. The priority given to autonomy over solidarity is the practical political and social outcome of this assumption. It has led inexorably to a significant diminishment of our sense of a life in common, because autonomy "is incapable of uniting . . . people". "To acknowledge either conscience or religion in any serious fashion is to reject the very idea of radical autonomy",[10] which is one of the reasons why both are increasingly intolerable to contemporary liberal democracy and the moral commitments which define it.

Freedom of religion and freedom of conscience both point beyond the autonomy of the individual to something that has a greater claim, whether transcendent or social. They recall us to the reality of our condition; that we are not gods but dependent creatures who need to be embedded in communities if the great freedom we enjoy is to be fruitful and enable us to flourish. Autonomy cannot provide a sustainable basis for a future or for justice, and the contradictions, absurdities and intolerance that have come to characterise the project founded upon it suggest disintegration. Seen in this light, the war on faith that Dyson Heydon describes may reflect not strength and assurance but a dawning awareness of things slipping away. We shall see. In any case, it is a war which still has some way to run.

5

A FUNDAMENTAL RIGHT UNDER THREAT

Peter Kurti

"The public voices of modern elites are not humble. They conceive themselves to have entitlements and rights, not blessings. And they do not feel any gratitude to Almighty God for their entitlements and rights," Dyson Heydon declared in his inaugural PM Glynn Lecture.

Instances of a fevered determination to uphold virtuous standards of conduct and thought among citizens are not hard to find in contemporary Australia. One of the most egregious forms of 'secular sin' that offends against these standards is discrimination on the basis of race, gender or sexual identity.

When Israel Folau, the Wallabies superstar, expressed his opinions about homosexuality in the autumn of 2018, he provoked a storm of protest from the *bien pensants* in the media, as well as from the self-appointed corporate guardians of public morality such as Qantas.[1] Folau, a devout Christian, was accused of hateful and discriminatory speech, but he was simply expressing the teachings upheld by the church to which he belongs—the Assemblies of God.

People were entirely free to agree or disagree with Folau; but if Australia is a genuinely free country, should he not have been quite free to express his genuinely held religious beliefs? And if our country is genuinely tolerant, should not Folau, and others who share his theological views, be free to say what they think, even though many will disagree with what they say?

The expression of different and, at times, controversial opinions and beliefs, however, is becoming harder. One of the reasons for this is that securing equality in all human relationships and social interactions has become a principal goal of many policy and legislative initiatives in

Australia, often imposed by the force of law. Some notion of 'diversity' is propounded whilst, at the same time, the real and unavoidable *differences* between human beings are denied or excluded.

The drive to legislate for various kinds of non-discriminatory behaviour began under the Whitlam Government with the passage of the *Racial Discrimination Act 1975*. It drew upon the International Covenant on Civil and Political Rights 1966 (ICCPR) to which Australia is a signatory.[2] Intended as a means to eradicate racism, the Racial Discrimination Act has become the cornerstone of Australia's multicultural policy. Its principles have set the tone for subsequent debates about equality and social inclusion.[3]

Religion and the concomitant requirements of anti-discrimination law present Australia with competing and conflicting demands. Even though formal participation in religious institutions in this country appears to be declining, the contribution they make to society remains strong.[4] Notwithstanding the place that religion clearly continues to occupy in Australian society, there is a lively debate about the extent to which it should do so.

Few, if any, in a liberal state, would mount an argument for religious intolerance or the removal of freedom to practise one's religion in peace. Religious liberty, however, is under attack in other and more insidious ways. Believers are under constant pressure to demonstrate that religious belief is a positive and, indeed, legitimate feature of liberal society. Those whose beliefs lead them to certain moral convictions are very likely to find themselves in conflict with secular culture. For many, it has become increasingly difficult to give public expression to moral positions informed by faith.

It is clearly the case that people are free to believe whatever they like—that the moon is made of cheese, say. There is little that any legislature can do to regulate what thoughts and beliefs people hold in their heads. Freedom of religion, therefore, must always be about more than internally held beliefs: it must be about the external practice and manifestation of belief.

The freedom to believe must always be accompanied by the freedom to speak and by the freedom to associate or dissociate. A concomitant characteristic of freedom of religion is the absence of coercion or constraint.[5] Both the behaviour and the conduct of believers are important in examining the scope of religious liberty because it is a freedom that may be conceived both in terms of free choice and assumed duty in response to a divine command. Religious freedom is, at the very least, the freedom given to a believer to fulfil that duty.[6] Most definitions of religious freedom begin with, or at least take into account, that set out in the United Nations Universal Declaration of Human Rights 1948 (the Universal Declaration). It includes the freedom to believe and disbelieve, and the freedom to refuse to participate in religious practice.[7]

The Universal Declaration recognises that the purely personal freedom of individuals to believe or think whatever they like is beyond the reach of the state. But it does define two external freedoms: first, a positive religious liberty whereby an individual enjoys the social freedom to manifest belief in private and in public; and, second, a negative religious liberty whereby an individual enjoys freedom from coercion or discrimination on the grounds of religious belief. The negative liberty was articulated in the ICCPR, which set out a specific freedom from coercion. The ICCPR also permits the state to set limitations to religious freedom, although this applies only to the external expression of belief and not, generally, to personal freedom of belief.[8]

The Universal Declaration and the ICCPR are two of the principal treaties setting out protections of religious freedom. Both have been ratified by Australia. Ratification entails a legal obligation to act consistently with the treaty but it does not automatically make the treaty provisions part of Australian law. Nor does it create rights that are directly enforceable in Australian courts. Indeed, such treaties do not form part of Australian law unless they are specifically included in legislation by the Commonwealth Parliament.

Furthermore, ratification of a treaty dealing with religious freedom confers no automatic power upon the Commonwealth Parliament to legislate for that freedom. This is because neither religion nor human rights falls under the heads of power that confer legislative power upon Parliament.[9] And should Parliament choose to legislate to protect religious freedom, it must be careful not to breach the constitutional prohibition and protection of religion as set out in section 116 of the Constitution, and which Michael Crennan discusses in detail in his contribution to this volume.[10]

Victoria and the ACT are the only two Australian jurisdictions that have introduced statutory protections of human rights, including the right to religious freedom.[11] Both the Victorian Charter and the ACT's *Human Rights Act 2004* require courts to interpret legislation in ways that are consistent with the provisions of the acts. Both acts contain very similar provisions prohibiting discrimination on the grounds of religion and establish a right to religious freedom.[12]

Legislation is one way of protecting religious freedom. Another, probably more convenient way of doing so is for the state to leave matters of religious life and practice unregulated. This approach allows individuals and communities the freedom to decide for themselves how best to organise matters of life and practice. The question of religious freedom will, however, still arise sharply in the event that the secular law commands certain forms of conduct that religious believers find unconscionable.

Religious beliefs are increasingly coming into conflict with the prevailing anti-discrimination *zeitgeist*. The reservations of religious believers are often dismissed by those who argue that issues such as equality, diversity and inclusiveness must prevail whenever they come into conflict with religious liberty.[13] Religious believers who hold such beliefs are frequently attacked and their liberty compromised in the name of tolerance. It remains one of the most prominent issues in contemporary debate about freedom of religion.

This clash continues to provoke controversy because it raises two linked issues: first, the extent to which religious believers should be free to manifest their religion and, second, the extent to which religious freedom should be accommodated by the requirements of anti-discrimination laws.

What the liberal state can and should do is secure the freedom of religious believers to live their lives in accordance with their beliefs so long as they do so in ways that do not undermine social cohesion. Any discussion of the right to freedom of religion needs to be mindful of the place that that right occupies in a larger quartet of freedoms.

Religious belief is not something that can be confined to the realm of the mind as though it were a kind of mental recreation. Belief and practice are inseparable; freedom to believe must surely be accompanied by the freedom to speak. Those whose ways of life are guided by the search for ultimate meaning and a solemn obligation to do so dutifully are often likely to clash with the values of the secular state.

It is not difficult to see that if this dutiful living is met with the coercive force of the state, not only the right to freedom of religion but also the broader rights of freedom of association and freedom of expression—part of the fabric of the liberal state—are bound to be put at risk.

This is not to call for state-backed guarantees of the credibility of a religious creed; it is simply to accept the right to believe what you want and to act on that belief in any way that does not threaten the peaceful social order. After all, religious believers are not the only ones who can behave in ways that cause offence and distress. Yet it is religious liberty that is now under threat, and liberal tolerance of religion that is waning in Western societies.

In a celebrated essay, the Harvard philosopher Michael Sandel argued that any consideration of the nature of religious freedom required making an important distinction between freedom of conscience and freedom of choice. He argues that whereas conscience dictates, choice decides: "Religious liberty [addresses] the problem of encumbered selves, claimed by duties they cannot renounce, even in the face of civil obligations that may conflict."[14]

One of the significant marks of the liberal state has been a readiness to recognise this burden borne by the encumbered. Such recognition has been both in terms of the moral worthiness of a life lived according to a higher authority and of the importance of allowing all citizens the freedom to act according to the demands of conscience. Questions about the scope of the freedom of religion enjoyed by encumbered selves can arise in various ways.

For instance, it may arise in the event that religious believers argue that compliance with their religious and moral code violates the secular law, or that the moral code articulated by their faith should be enforced by the secular law and imposed upon non-adherents. Other questions will arise if religious groups demand exemption from taxation or from building codes or from specific legal protections prohibiting criticism of beliefs, or if they claim entitlement to refuse employment to members of minority groups.

Needless to say, a claim by one group to religious freedom may just as readily be viewed by another as a claim to religious privilege. It is in precisely this way that conflict can arise between religious believers and non-adherents as well as with the state. Since rival claims about the manifestation of a supernatural realm in the natural realm are not readily verified or falsified, such conflicts defy resolution.[15]

Protections long afforded by the liberal state to those bearing the claim of Sandel's unrenounceable duties, however, are now being threatened by the contemporary corrective tendency to minimise cultural differences as a way of managing diversity. This tendency, powered by the legislative fuel of anti-discrimination laws, promotes minority identity to the status of an end in itself.

Although passed with the intention of inhibiting intolerance, anti-discrimination laws have effectively pursued equality by removing from the public sphere all that distinguishes one group of citizens from another. Whether these distinguishing factors are religious forms of address or the performance of public roles and rituals, their removal serves only to undermine the very diversity and tolerance the legislation purports to promote, thereby inhibiting the freedom of all citizens.

Patrick Parkinson has noted that if it is to contribute to the health of our society, anti-discrimination legislation must be framed so as to improve the capacity of minority communities who share a particular faith or ethnicity to strengthen the bonds that join them together and thereby flourish: "The issue is what freedom minority communities need at the margin in order to build the cohesiveness of their own groups according to the values that bind them together."[16] Why the concern with the margins of religious freedom? In Parkinson's view, the margin defines the minimum scope of freedom required by religious groups "to build cohesiveness according to the values that bind them together."[17]

In an important article published in the *Monash University Law Review*, Parkinson and Harrison have identified a more recent shift in the focus of anti-discrimination law. Instead of an emphasis on cohesion grounded in the shared values of the group, Parkinson and Harrison argue that this new focus is on protecting an individual's identity and that it represents a shift towards the maximisation of different lifestyles: "Discrimination law, on this account, centres more on respect for, and facilitation of, personal autonomy, or attempting to reduce the costs to individuals of adhering to certain identities."[18]

Parkinson and Harrison have re-examined the way in which the boundaries of religious association might be described, defining, in turn, the areas where anti-discrimination law should apply. They employ the concept of the 'commons' to determine boundaries of a sphere within which no member of a community can expect to be excluded. It goes far beyond a simple distinction between public and private but embraces public authority and enterprise.[19]

Beyond the commons, however, Parkinson and Harrison argue there lies a range of groups and organisations which bring together those who share opinions, interests, and experiences. It is by their internal norms that these groups ought to be free to regulate their ways of life.[20] The boundary of the 'commons' is a valuable concept for describing those arenas of social and community life within which difference can be acknowledged not only to exist but also to matter.

The majority culture may neither accept nor even like the traditions of those arenas; nonetheless, they need to be recognised as part of the fabric of social associations which go to make up the wider community. Within the 'commons', however, the norms of anti-discrimination law must apply: "the law, in other words, continues to play an important general role in establishing standards within communal spaces."[21]

The contribution of Parkinson and Harrison is significant because it takes seriously the existence of all kinds of differences between people and groups; and it acknowledges that these differences matter. Yet living in the area beyond the 'commons' does not obviate the need for these groups to exist and engage with one another. This, they argue, is "consistent with multicultural Australia, its plural sources of authority, and principles of religious liberty."[22]

When governments attempt to manipulate these differences by imposing laws that enforce a particular conception of social life and behaviour, they threaten to turn difference, whether cultural, social, intellectual or economic, into a moral entity to which an obligation of fairness in the pursuit of equality is then owed.

But it is impossible for a diverse society to be one in which everyone is trying equally hard to achieve the same goals. To argue that democracy should seek the obliteration of difference is to adopt a statist form of liberalism that has only an attenuated view of the freedom enjoyed by the open-minded liberal citizen to express his or her own interests and beliefs. Indeed, it conflicts with the very ideal of religious belief where the search for truth requires open-minded enquiry.

The political and cultural framework of the liberal state needs to allow believers and non-believers alike, with differing and even conflicting points of view, to live together peacefully. In other words, citizens of the state need to enjoy equal standing before the law without expecting identical treatment.

The liberal state does not coerce its citizens to adopt one worldview or set of beliefs, for to do so would be to impose a tyranny of tolerance. Differing outlooks must be allowed to co-exist unless the safety and well-being of those citizens is put in jeopardy.

The crucial point is that when the liberal state does act to restrict freedom of speech, it ought not to do so to protect religious sensibilities or to defend religious traditions of belief and conduct, but simply to protect the secular, or worldly, interests of the state itself, and the liberty of all its citizens.

'Secular' is a word that can mean many things. It is, however, an appropriate word to describe a political philosophy or outlook that is neutral as to the existence or relevance of a religious dimension in public affairs.

In a lecture delivered in 2006, the then Archbishop of Canterbury, Rowan Williams, identified two forms of secularism.[23] One form, 'procedural secularism', recognises the importance of religion to its citizens and permits equal participation in the public sphere while refraining from imposing any religious beliefs.

Another version of secularism, however, contends that the state should no longer refrain from imposing belief but should actively establish unbelief as the norm. In contrast with procedural secularism, 'programmatic secularism' holds that there can be no place at all in the public sphere for any non-material or supernatural account of human life.[24]

The emergence of programmatic secularism has been accompanied by a willingness on the part of the state to use its legislative powers to diminish and even exclude the influence of religion in shaping public policy. It is part of the process that Raymond Plant describes as the transition of liberal democracy from *ethos* (a matter of practice and habit) to rules and explicit principles.

Whereas *ethos* allows for fudging and compromises between different points of view, "making liberal principles explicit in law means greatly reducing the scope for easy fudging and compromise."[25] As religious voices count for less in public policy debates, religious groups are, in time, denied the exemptions that embody religious freedom.

To say that secularism is neutral to the existence of religion in society is not to say it is impartial to the impact or effect it has on that society. Burdens have been added to the free practice of religious belief by the elision of procedural secularism into programmatic secularism. At its worst, this imposition has created a climate that has been actively hostile to the liberty enjoyed by religious believers. Nonetheless, advocates of burdensome legislation argue that it is intended to uphold the virtue of civic equality as a basic feature of liberal democracy.

Secular virtues, such as equality, are nowadays being imposed with aggressive assertiveness by the state in the name of tolerance and dignity. This pursuit of inoffensiveness effectively imposes a tyranny of tolerance upon the individual citizen. This tyranny, in turn, threatens the freedoms the citizen has long enjoyed under the liberal state to pursue his or her conception of the good life, especially the right to religious liberty.

Since religion involves the human pursuit of ultimate meaning and value, it is not far-fetched to argue that erosion of religious liberty impedes pursuit of a higher purpose that can contribute significantly to deep human fulfilment and satisfaction. This pursuit, however, will not necessarily occur without generating some degree of conflict.

Wrangling about questions of ultimate meaning among adherents of different religions is almost certainly bound to cause offense in a diverse modern Western society. It is hard to see any realistic way to defang religion of this potential for offence since each group's creed may well seem like an outrage to every other group.[26] Conduct that manifests a creed is also likely to offend, but if the questions are important, the state needs to enshrine and uphold the right to religious freedom as a fundamental liberal right.

A person may come to a religiously informed and sincerely held conviction that policy positions advocated by other people (such as same-sex marriage, physician-assisted suicide, or abortion) are morally repugnant. Once a religious believer acts upon that conviction, whether in speech or in print or by peaceful protest, offence is bound to be caused to those who disagree. Protections under the rule of law must be extended, nonetheless, to those who cause such offence—something very different from defending protections for those who incite hatred or violence towards others.

Yet the social forces of exclusion have been mobilised against religious believers in Australia. For advocates of militant secularism, such as the Australian Greens, this is unexceptional and is to be considered part of the price worth paying in the pursuit of a society characterised by their particular conceptions of the qualities of 'equality' and 'dignity'. It is a dangerous development, however; one that falls into the error of hard secularism where non-religious and religious discourse are set in direct and antagonistic opposition to one another.

No fair-minded and free-thinking citizen should advocate hatred of, or discrimination against, another person on the basis of ethnicity, gender, sexual orientation or belief. The problem, however, is that where such advocacy does occur, it is met both by counter-argument, social ostracism, and even bullying—and, increasingly, by immediate recourse to the law.

Rights and freedoms recognised in a liberal society must be capable of coexisting and being recognised together. The drive to eradicate all forms of discrimination is gathering such momentum, however, shaped, as it is by the forces of identity politics, that it threatens to eradicate the right to religious liberty into the bargain, along with many other forms of diversity, variety and difference.

Once claims about discriminatory behaviour or beliefs are presented as assaults upon the person, they become non-negotiable. Demands for tolerance give way, as Dyson Heydon observed, to demands for unconditional surrender. Developments such as this will only make it harder, in the long run, for Australian society to be authentically tolerant of difference and disagreement.

6

CHURCH-STATE RELATIONS IN RECENT HISTORY

M. J. Crennan

Dyson Heydon's trenchant inaugural PM Glynn Lecture raises many issues about religion, law and public life. He has set out many things about modern life of which he is critical, and he makes a strong case that many of them are to some degree interconnected. I have chosen to discuss the question, at the heart of his lecture, of the way in which the courts and the legislature have mediated church-state relations in the last few centuries.

I have attempted to give a general overview of the free exercise and anti-establishment clauses contained in the First Amendment of the American Constitution and section 116 of our own Constitution. After briskly surveying this historical field, I shall try to draw together some observations about more immediately contemporary problems in the light of what has gone before. I shall try to sketch the present state of statutory law in respect of the issue of religious liberty. I respectfully agree with Dyson Heydon that there is insufficient protection of liberty of thought and communication at present, although that might alter. Although I discuss both the free exercise and anti-establishment clauses, central to my thesis is that the American jurisprudence of the latter is not directly relevant to Australian conditions but, for reasons I shall attempt to explain, is quite relevant to some broader questions about the way religion, and its demands on the informed conscience, are addressed in recent case law.

From the late eighteenth century to the early twentieth century a number of Western nation-states developed constitutional, customary, legislative and jurisprudential arrangements and doctrines, aimed at regulating the relationship of church and state. In these reflections two of them will be discussed: the United States and Australia (the order is chronological). In each case there are two classes of provisions regarding religion, generally known as the 'free exercise clause', and the 'anti-establishment clause'. A related tension also exists between religious freedom and the sanctions of the general, particularly the criminal, law. It is convenient to set out the relevant clauses at the outset.

Amendment I of the Constitution of the United States provides:

> Congress shall make no law respecting an establishment of religion, or prohibiting the exercise thereof, or abridging the freedom of speech, or of the press, or the right of the people peaceably to assemble, and to petition the Government for a redress of grievances.

Section 116 of the Australian Constitution provides:

> The Commonwealth shall not make any law for establishing any religion, or for imposing any religious observance, or for prohibiting the free exercise of any religion, and no religious test shall be required as a qualification for any office or public trust under the Commonwealth.

The anti-establishment clauses differ significantly. The American article forbids any law "respecting an establishment of religion", and the Australian provision, more directly, forbids any law "for" establishing a religion (in other words, a law which has that purpose).[1] As we shall see, in practice, the American courts have taken their anti-establishment clause to be sufficiently breached by treating a church *as if it were* an established church and, accordingly, the detection of any of the incidents of that status is one of the several indicia in deciding whether the dealings between church and state in question are prohibited. This catches a much wider range of conduct than the Australian clause, and the immense literature on the American clause reflects that fact.

The Constitution of the United States was conceived by founders deeply read in both Classical and Enlightenment learning, not always sympathetic to religion. The societies of the founding States had a significant degree of confessional diversity, many constituent groups of which had a strong cohesion born of persecution and consequent flight to the refuge they believed the western hemisphere could offer them. Some States had established churches (that is, churches with a privileged relation to the secular authorities),[2] others did not. A successful war of independence had been prosecuted against Britain, and the Constitution reflected a buoyant sense of possibility and mission, whatever tensions or disputes may have preceded, or even continued beyond, the final form of the document. It was signed by forty-two delegates of the States in September 1787. Its preamble sets out the values and aspirations of the new nation, in this order: Unity, Justice, domestic tranquillity, defence, general welfare, and Liberty (I follow the capitalisation in the original).[3] Rounding out the democratic programme were the ten Amendments, now known as the Bill of Rights, ratified in December 1791. The very first such Amendment deals *inter alia* with religion. It is notable that the First Amendment deals with four other freedoms, whereas section 116 of the Australian Constitution deals only with religion, but with more particularity than the First Amendment.

The subject matter of disputes about the meaning of the anti-establishment clause of the First Amendment has included religious instruction in public schools, school prayers, bible readings in public schools, financial and other aid to parochial schools, opening prayers in the legislature, the problem of 'entanglement' and religious observance in prisons. The free exercise clause cases have included disputes over polygamy, conscientious objections, saluting the flag, Sabbatarian cases, oaths, unemployment cases, and anti-evolution laws.

General statements of principle have been made but must be treated warily. In *Everson v Board of Education*,[4] the Supreme Court had to consider a statute which authorised school boards to provide funds for the transport of schoolchildren, including those attending Catholic schools. Justice Black enunciated the following test: proscribed are "laws which aid one religion, and all religions, or prefer one religion over another. No tax in any amount, large or small, can be levied to support any religious activities or institutions. . . . In the words of Jefferson, the establishment clause was meant to erect 'a wall of separation between church and state'".[5] Because, in this case, the law provided necessary services to *all* schoolchildren, it was neutral and therefore did not fall foul of the First Amendment.

Sixteen years later, Justice Black had to consider another application of the anti-establishment clause in *Engel v Vitale*.[6] A public school had its students recite a non-denominational prayer. The Supreme Court held that the practice violated the clause: there was no protection against children being converted to a religious belief; there might arise a peer pressure to convert to a religious belief. This resembled the French doctrine of *laïcité*, to the effect that the school is to be a public place where the student is to be protected from religious recruitment or even exposure, whether by activities, instruction, or prominent display of religious images and the like. This principle has no application to the private space of home, for instance. It is the principle on which the French anti-concealment law is said to be based.

In 1948, in *McCollum v Board of Education*,[7] it was held that voluntary religious lessons requiring parental approval were prohibited, because the lessons were held on premises provided out of state revenues, and that the children were on the premises as a result of the State's requirement of compulsory attendance. In the case of *Zorach v Clauson*, it was held, on the other hand, that classes held away from school did not necessarily breach the clause.

The same activity might be permissible when pursued for one purpose, but not if pursued for another. To read the Bible as part of a history project would not offend the clause, whereas reading it for the purpose of religious education would.[8]

The character of the school could be taken into account. Early education was a case in point. In parochial schools in particular it has been held that it was impossible to distinguish lay from religious content, and therefore the clause was enlivened. One leading case gave rise to a three-part test which has not uniformly been followed in later cases.[9] The questions to be addressed are:

- Is the purpose secular or religious?
- Is the principal effect either to advance or inhibit religion? (Both are prohibited).

- Is the activity one which will tend to create a situation where the government finds itself excessively entangled with religion?

Some decisions are not easy to reconcile with a rational interpretation of the provision. For example, the legislature of Nebraska had, since 1855, opened its daily session with a prayer. The Supreme Court cautioned, while permitting the practice, that the long-standing nature of a practice in itself would not save it from constitutional challenge.[10] In a later case, the challenge succeeded in relation to a graduation ceremony on the basis that it was not easy to leave the ceremony.

Turning to the free exercise clause, we see a number of cases include problems which arise from the diversity of religious regimes in the nineteenth century. Some religious groups, for example, practised polygamy, or refused to salute the flag on the ground that to do so was a form of idolatry. In dealing with some of these situations, the Supreme Court laid down the critical principle that the holder of a religious belief cannot rely on that belief to excuse behaviour which is otherwise a breach of the criminal law.

It is reasonably clear that to make out a conscientious objection a claimant must demonstrate a conscientious belief that *all* war is wrong, not merely the conflict of the day. Other, more complicated scenarios are, however, possible. In 1946, a pacifist migrant from Canada wished to obtain American citizenship. In order to do so, he had to swear that, if called upon, he would defend the United States. This seemed to be an obstacle to taking the oath, without which he could not become a citizen. However, the Supreme Court held that the oath would be satisfied by non-combatant service, so the path to the oath, and thus citizenship, remained open.[11]

In 1890, Mr Davis, a Mormon, found that, in order to obtain voter status, he was obliged to take an oath in what was then the Territory of Idaho to the effect that he did not support polygamy, nor did he belong to an organisation that did so. Plainly he could not swear the oath. It was held that the restriction of the voting qualification was valid, and that he could not rely on the free exercise clause, because of various public interest considerations.[12] Seventy-one years later, however, in the case of *Torcaso v Watkins*,[13] the Supreme Court, applying the free exercise clause, struck down a requirement of the State of Maryland that in order to become a notary the applicant had to affirm a belief in the existence of God.

Three comparatively recent decisions of the Supreme Court shed some light on the current state of the law in the United States dealing with church-state relations.

In *Hosanna-Tabor Evangelical Lutheran Church and School v Equal Employment Commission et al*,[14] the Court had to consider the so-called ministerial exception and the operation of the *Americans with Disabilities Act*. The ministerial exception was to the effect that both the free exercise and anti-establishment clauses "bar the government from interfering with the decision of a religious group to fire one of its ministers". The church in question was a member of the second largest Lutheran Congregation in the United States. It ran a school in Redford, Michigan. Teachers could be lay teachers or 'called' teachers. Called teachers had to undergo an examination and certification process, after which they could be 'called' by the congregation, and would then be described, and held out to the public, as ministers. Sheryl Petrich went through this process and taught at the school for several years as a called teacher. She became ill in 2004, with narcolepsy. She was unable to teach for some time, but eventually presented herself to the school, with medical evidence of fitness, to resume work. The school did not wish to re-employ her, which she did not accept. Eventually, she brought an action against the school under the *Americans with Disabilities Act*. She claimed that the Church had discriminated against her. This was the first such case before the Supreme Court brought on that basis. The Court found that she was in truth a minister. She sought reinstatement from the Court but abandoned that claim. As Chief Justice Roberts pointed out, "By requiring the Church to accept a minister it did not want, such an order would have plainly violated the Church's freedom under the religion clauses to select its own ministers". An order for compensation was also disallowed because, in order to grant it, the Court would have to examine the reasoning behind the Church's decision, which was not permissible.

The last paragraph of the Chief Justice's opinion places a strong emphasis on the protection of religious liberty: "The interest of society in the enforcement of employment discrimination statutes is undoubtedly important. But so too is the interest of religious groups in choosing who will preach their beliefs, teach their faith, and carry out their mission".

The Trinity Lutheran Church Child Learning Center was a childcare and early learning centre. The Missouri Government offered grants to schools to pay for a product derived from recycled tyres to be used in resurfacing playgrounds and the like. The Learning Center needed such resurfacing and applied for a grant. It was refused. The relevant authority advised that any application for a grant was to be refused if made by a church, because of Article I, Section 7 of the Missouri Constitution, which reads:

> That no money shall ever be taken from the public treasury, directly or indirectly in aid of any church, sect or denomination of religion, or in aid of any priest, preacher, minister or teacher thereof, as such; and no preference shall be given to nor any discrimination made against any church, sect, or creed of religion, or any form of religious faith or worship.

In its opinion, delivered by Chief Justice Roberts, the Supreme Court made reference to a number of earlier decisions, in which "this Court has repeatedly confirmed that denying a generally available benefit solely on account of religious identity imposes a penalty on the free exercise of religion that can be justified only by a state interest 'of the highest order'." It distinguished recent cases where it had rejected free exercise claims because "the laws in question [were] neutral and generally applicable without regard to religion. We have been careful to distinguish such laws from those that single out the religious for disfavoured treatment". Here Trinity Lutheran Church Child Learning Center could not compete for a benefit generally available *only because* it was a religious institution. Justice Sotomayr, joined by Justice Ginsburg, tackles the majority in fine detail, but it provides a lesson in the passion and conviction underlying the Court's differences, and for that reason its concluding paragraph merits quotation:

> History shows that the Religion Clauses separate the public treasury from religious coffers as one measure to secure the kind of freedom of conscience that benefits both religion and government. If this separation means anything, it means that the government cannot, or at the very least need not, tax its citizens and turn that money over to houses of worship. The Court today blinds itself to the outcome this history requires and leads us instead to a place where separation of church and state is a constitutional slogan, not a constitutional commitment. I dissent.

The ructions caused by the Lutheran toddlers of Boone County, Missouri, fade in comparison with the next case. On June 30, 2014, the Supreme Court decided the case of *Burwell, Secretary of Health and Human Services et al v Hobby Lobby Stores Inc*.[15] The proprietors of Hobby Lobby, a closely held company, operating a large chain of shops selling craft materials and the like, refused to support a government programme, which could entail the provision of morning-after contraceptives, which they believed to be a form of abortion. Serious financial penalties were prescribed for this refusal. Two other companies joined Hobby Lobby, on identical grounds.

The three groups relied upon the *Religious Freedom Restoration Act* of 1993, which provides that "Government shall not substantially burden a person's exercise of religion *even if* the burden results from a rule of general applicability". The Act, furthermore, provided a statutory test, which required the government to prove that the rule objected to:

- is in furtherance of a compelling interest; *and* (my emphasis)
- is the least restrictive means of furthering that compelling government interest.

The second condition is a statutory creation, not previously a part of the tests applied by the Court. The case in large measure turned on it. Specific exemptions were available to religious bodies, and the like, but this did not cover any of the applicants, who were lay people. The relevant regulations were made under a statute called the *Patient Protection and Affordable Care Act* (2010). This Act provides that an employer who does not provide the insurance as required will incur very severe financial penalties. The three groups sought the protection of the general exemption.

An objection that the companies were not able to exercise religion (and therefore could not have that non-existent exercise burdened) was given short shrift, the Court holding that, for the purpose of the free exercise clause, the rights and protections given to companies were in truth given to the natural persons who owned, operated, were officers of, or employed by them. The action of the government was a burden to the claimants. It placed the claimants in the position that, in order to exercise their religion, i.e. by declining to facilitate the supply of contraceptives which they believed to be abortifacients, they would be burdened with a very large financial penalty, in the tens of millions of dollars in the case of Hobby Lobby. Putting it another way, the conduct of the companies they controlled was a matter of conscience for their proprietors. Without those people the company can do nothing. Any moral wrongs the companies committed were to be laid at the feet, and burdened the conscience, of the proprietors and, since this conscience sprang from their religious beliefs, to force the people involved to bear that burden by the threat of financial penalties, whether successful or not, was to burden the exercise of their religion.[16]

Other arguments about the standing and nature of companies were likewise dismissed. An argument that the legislation merely codified an earlier understanding of the First Amendment jurisprudence was vigorously rejected.

The Department of Health and Human Services argued that, given the remoteness in time and causality between supplying the insurance and any embryo-destruction, the connection is too attenuated. The Supreme Court responded in its majority opinion, delivered by Justice Alito, that this is no more than investigating the reasonableness of the sincerely held belief, which is not open to it in cases of free exercise.

The Court declined to adjudicate the first issue (whether there was a compelling government interest). They proceeded on the basis that there was such an interest, but found that this was immaterial because the second prong of the test—the 'least restrictive' test—had not been satisfied. The Court observed that this test is "exceptionally demanding". The Court was critical of the failure of the Department to provide any evidence on a number of possible alternatives. There already existed a programme which would enable the insurance to be obtained, without the involvement of Hobby Lobby or the other firms or their respective proprietors. This was an accommodation by which a non-profit *religious* organisation could certify that the supply of contraceptives would violate its religious tenets, at which the insurance issuer or third-party administrator would be required to exclude contraceptives from the plan and provide separate payments for any contraceptive services to be provided without imposing any cost-sharing requirements on a number of relevant bodies. In order to satisfy the imperatives of the free exercise clause, such an accommodation was to be provided to the claimants. This effectively gave the individuals in question rights similar to the statutory rights afforded to religious organisations.

Justice Ginsburg's dissent is spirited and detailed. Her comments about the social programme, of which the arrangements considered in this case form a part, show deep familiarity with the background to the legislation, not to mention a deep commitment to the needs of women. Her comments about the rather blasé way in which the majority devise a solution to the problems of a dozen or so rich people by inconveniencing large numbers of less fortunate workers (if accurate), and women in particular, are resonant. Nonetheless, the majority, narrow as it was (5:4), firmly rejected any application of the corporate veil, or any other matters raised in the submissions made, in matters arising from the free exercise clause. In so doing they gave primacy to the authority of the free exercise clause, well over that of the countervailing considerations. This is the true heart of the case, and one which jurists, not confined to the United States, may have to address for some time to come, as has been made evident in recent months in the Masterpiece Cakeshop decision of the American Supreme Court.[17]

The authors of the Australian Constitution had a very different base from which to work. Australia maintained close relations with the United Kingdom. The Australian Constitution was to be a predominantly practical rather than an aspirational document. The society to which the founders looked—the United Kingdom—had provided an example, over the preceding century, of gradual, and largely peaceful extension of civic rights to its Jewish, non-conformist and Catholic citizens. One consequence was that the interpretation, and not only the content, of apparently similar constitutional provisions relating to religion developed along a different path in Australia.

In 1912, the free exercise clause was considered by the High Court. The Defence Act required that, with some exceptions, all male inhabitants of Australia who were British subjects should undergo military training. An appellant to the High Court claimed that he was not liable to undergo training because of his religious beliefs.[18] The Court found that section 116 of the Australian Constitution did not apply. It concerns only laws which prohibit "the practice of religion—the doing of acts which are done in the practice of religions. To require a man to do an act which his religion forbids would be objectionable on moral grounds, but it does not come within the prohibition of section 116".[19] Furthermore, one exception under the Act was that persons liable to undergo training "who are forbidden by the doctrines of their religion to bear arms shall as far as possible be allotted to non-combatant duties". In the light of that exception the Court held that the appellant's claim to be exempted must fail, in any event. The interpretation of the free exercise clause found in this case is curt and narrow.

In 1943, the Court had to consider this question:

> Does section 116 prevent the Commonwealth Parliament from legislating to restrain the activities of a body, the existence of which is, in the opinion of the Governor-General, prejudicial to the defence of the Commonwealth or the efficient prosecution of the war, if that body is a religious organisation? Is the answer to this question affected by the fact that the subversive activities of such a body are founded upon the religious views of its members? Can such a body be suppressed?[20]

In addressing these questions, the Chief Justice enunciated a number of principles:

- ". . . no law can escape the application of section 116 simply because it is a law which can be justified under sections 51 or 52, or under some other head of legislative power. All the legislative powers of the Commonwealth are subject to the condition which section 116 imposes".

- Section 116 applies to all religions.

- Section 116 applies to all the characteristics of a religion, at least including its system of beliefs, its doctrines, its code of conduct, its ritual or religious observance. "Section 116 must be regarded as operating in relation to all these aspects of religion".

- Section 116 applies equally to the right to have no religion.

- Section 116 applies to acts "done in pursuance of religious belief as part of religion".

- Belief in a Supreme Being may not be an essential attribute of religion (e.g. Buddhism).

- The attributes of religion are not a closed category: "each person chooses the content of his own religion. It is not for a court, upon some a priori basis, to disqualify certain beliefs as incapable of being religious in character".

- Some forms of conduct, while being in some sense religious, are impermissible under the criminal law. American jurisprudence had developed a doctrine that it is for the courts to determine "whether the freedom of religion has been 'unduly' infringed". This test could legally be adopted by Australian courts.

- In the present case, however, the Chief Justice preferred to adopt a narrower test based on the principle that "the protection of any form of liberty as a social right within a society necessarily involves the continued existence of that society as a society".

- The use of the word "for" in the section requires that the purpose of the legislation must be determined by the Court.

- The other members of the Court agreed in the Chief Justice's reasons, in whole or in part.

In 1981, the High Court heard an important case dealing with the anti-establishment clause brought by a group known as DOGS (Defence of Government Schools) which sought a ruling that the introduction of state aid to religious (mainly Catholic) schools was unconstitutional in that it offended section 116 of the Constitution.[21]

Some significant parts of the judgments include:

- Section 116 applies to all laws of the Commonwealth.
- The word 'for' necessarily means that the establishment of a church must be the purpose of the legislation in order to violate section 116. Effect or tendency is not enough. This distinguishes the American jurisprudence from the Australian.
- The Chief Justice explained that relevant characteristics of an established church are: "the entrenchment of a religion as a feature of and identified with the body politic, in this instance the Commonwealth. It involves the identification of the religion with the civil authority so as to involve the citizen in a duty to maintain it and the obligation of, in this case the Commonwealth, to patronise, protect and promote the established religion". Justice Gibbs held that to establish a church meant in 1900 "to constitute a particular religion or religious body, as a state religion or state church". Justice Stephen proposed an effectively identical definition. Justice Mason preferred the formula "a national institution". Justice Murphy in dissent and, attempting to rely upon American precedent (he dismissed the difference in wording between the First Amendment and section 116 as "trifles of difference" and "hair-splitting"), held that section 116 means that the Commonwealth cannot "support religion in any way what-so-ever" and that "it forbids not only a national church and any preference to one religion over others, but also sponsorship and support (including financial support)". Justice Aickin agreed with Justices Gibbs and Mason. Justice Wilson agreed that establishment involved a church becoming a national institution.

This important case determined that the American and Australian anti-establishment clauses have crucially distinct meanings. In Australia, the section requires proof of a purpose to establish a church, which is unlikely ever to be found. In America, there is a multitude of tests in a multitude of combinations which might expose conduct to the operation of the First Amendment. That is the difference.

Section 116 of the Australian Constitution contains a free exercise clause. That section has been held to apply to all Commonwealth laws and to have a very broad scope. The exceptions noted by the High Court involve, in general, exceptionally grave circumstances, such as, for example, the destruction of, or at least a damaging attack on, the polity itself.[22] It follows that any Commonwealth legislation purporting to deny the rights conferred by section 116 without very grave reasons indeed would be liable to constitutional challenge. Section 116 is a constitutional guarantee of religious liberty, as regards the exercise of the legislative powers of the Commonwealth, although any attempt to define its scope must be qualified by the fact that the Australian jurisprudence on that section is quite undeveloped in comparison with that of the United States. One area which has caused concern is the advent of same-sex marriage. Protection of clergy and religious marriage celebrants and religious bodies, but not more generally, has been provided in sections 47(3), 47A(1) and 47B of the *Marriage Act 1961*:

> 47(3)—A minister of religion may refuse to solemnise a marriage despite anything in this Part, if any of the following applies:
> - the refusal conforms to the doctrines, tenets or beliefs of the religion of the minister's religious body or religious organisation;
> - the refusal is necessary to avoid injury to the religious susceptibilities of adherents of that religion;
> - the minister's religious beliefs do not allow the minister to solemnise the marriage.
>
> 47A(1)—A religious marriage celebrant may refuse to solemnise a marriage despite anything in this Part, if the celebrant's religious beliefs do not allow the celebrant to solemnise the marriage.

47B—A body established for religious purposes may refuse to make a facility available, or to provide goods or services, for the purposes of the solemnisation of a marriage, or for purposes reasonably incidental to the solemnisation of a marriage, if the refusal:

- conforms to the doctrines, tenets or beliefs of the religion of the body; or
- is necessary to avoid injury to the religious susceptibilities of adherents of that religion.

Victoria and the ACT have enacted legislation which has some of the character of a bill of rights, although, for the purposes of individual litigants, a toothless one for the moment.[23] Both statutes contain a provision about religious liberty. Section 14 of Victoria's *Charter of Human Rights and Responsibilities Act 2006* provides:

- Every person has the right to freedom of thought, conscience, religion and belief, including—
  - the freedom to have or to adopt a religion or belief of his or her choice; and
  - the freedom to demonstrate his or her religion or belief in worship, observance, practice and teaching, either individually or as part of a community, in public or in private.
- A person must not be coerced or restrained in a way that limits his or her freedom to have or adopt a religion or belief in worship.

One of the several concerns held on the issue of religious liberty is that, where church teaching may be offensive to the sensibilities of litigious persons or groups in the community, proceedings may be brought under Commonwealth legislation. Section 18C of the *Racial Discrimination Act 1975* is sometimes invoked in this discussion. Whilst this does not forbid discrimination against a person on the grounds of religious belief (as Dyson Heydon points out), it could, however, be employed to attack the teaching of a church on the grounds of allegedly offensive conduct.[24] It is most unlikely that such an occasion would arise, or, if it did arise, that the complaint would be well founded, and I do not suggest otherwise. The Victorian legislation refers to "the freedom to demonstrate his or her religion or belief in worship, observance, practice and teaching". This is a wide set of freedoms and would cover a number of the scenarios which have been envisaged. On the other hand, stating that such a freedom exists is a far cry from providing a remedy against the violation of that freedom, nor does it necessarily provide a defence to a claim made under other legislation (not to mention the section 109 issue which might arise in the case of Commonwealth legislation).

Would the free exercise provisions of section 116 of the Australian Constitution prevail, should the question ever arise, over section 18C of the Racial Discrimination Act, or, in the case of lay persons and bodies not covered by the exceptions in the Marriage Act, section 5A of the *Sex Discrimination Act 1984*? If Australian courts applied some of the generally stated principles set out in the Hobby Lobby case, the answer might well be "yes" in an appropriate case. But the relatively undeveloped jurisprudence on the issue in Australia precludes a confident prediction. If the Australian courts are at all moved to adopt the recent American approaches, some of the lacunae in the protection of religious liberty might be closed. Under the present legislative arrangements, however, and in the absence of reforms, section 116, limited as it is to Commonwealth legislation, may provide the only protection in some circumstances. Recent jurisprudence in the United States points the way to refreshing the original purpose of the free exercise clause, that is, to recognise the conscience of the citizen, guided by religious principles, as a strong component of some of the fundamental freedoms and values in our society. The Colorado baker's case demonstrates (but does not resolve) some of the difficult questions of balance which lie ahead for legislators, courts and other institutions and persons in the public realm. Good faith is required from all such institutions and from concerned citizens, but the solution does not lie in the abandonment of long recognised rights and values, and the silencing of religion.

7

A NEW CONSERVATIVE NARRATIVE

Hayden Ramsay

I remember the moment I realised narratives do exist outside story books. I had previously thought narrative a rather trendy, anti-realist notion in philosophy. That night—and it was some time ago and at another university—I sat through a speaker's presentation and understood that we cannot meaningfully make accusations of racism against black people or sexism against women. This is because of the narrative within which these concepts exist, find their established meaning and use, and the narrative history within which the concepts were clarified.

'Cannot' is a strong word, and in one perfectly clear sense we *can* make these comments, and many do. But such concepts as the '-isms' (sexism, racism . . .) derive their meaning and effect from a background worldview in which a specified group is systematically victimised by those who are not members of that group (women are treated unfairly by men, black people by white people). When men are treated unfairly by women that is wrong, and maybe very wrong indeed. But the wrong is not adequately described or explained as sexism. In fact, labelling it this way just puzzles as it connects the offence to assumptions and history that do not explain it. We cannot swap the sexes and keep the same wrong. This is partly because not all (or most or many) men are treated badly by women, and partly because when this does happen it happens for different reasons, against different assumptions and exhibits different types of character flaw and patterns of activity.

So incidents of women mistreating men may be as bad as sexism or worse, but are different from that vast social injustice through which women are routinely wrongly treated: female sexism does not fit the narrative. This thought does not feel particularly comfortable—or just, but if we try to oppose the narrative, the argument will fail pragmatically, i.e. it will not convince people, not be respected and may be counter-productive. It will also fail rhetorically, and perhaps even logically, for in attempting to make a point about general justice we are using a concept (the '-ism') which takes its meaning from a highly specific social context, i.e. it is a concept of special justice.

This point is linked to a type of reverse-argument popular with conservatives. A frequent conservative cry is: the accusers of intolerance are themselves highly intolerant; the victim class actually has power and uses it exploitatively; demands for equal treatment are in fact premised on an unequal view of human rights and priorities. Conservatives here exercise a balancing function in recalling that justice means treating like matters alike and that this often cuts across the cherished categories of identity politics. Some have a (quite rational) fear of joining this conservative critique—and then feel anxious and guilty that our silence helps entrench a form of inequality whereby those who identify with a victim-class are permitted to act in ways we would not tolerate from others.

Failure to allege female sexism, anti-Christian persecution, homosexual prejudice can induce these same feelings of anxiety and guilt. What are the alternatives? We may simply have to sit-out this narrative, but meantime we can look to future possibilities for a counter-narrative. On the radical account of human equality devised by classical and Christian wisdom, no one is victim by identity or class-membership alone but only by demonstration of intentional deprivation of or attack upon something fully necessary if we are to flourish as persons, i.e. by violation of our natural rights. We are presently awaiting a new narrative for this older wisdom.

Mr J. D. Heydon's Glynn Lecture explores elements of such a narra-tive. Classical learning, Christian faith, social conservatism and natural law jurisprudence are great friends and enjoy warm relationships. I rec-ognise that not everyone is equally comfortable with all partners in that relation. And when it comes down to it, my own view is that Christian faith—a gift from God that is cause of the worldview and choices of those who accept it—is the term in the relation that matters most. It is certainly possible for Christian faith to exist in ignorance of the classics, rejection of social conservatism and dismissal of the natural law. I think the resulting faith would be impoverished, harder to live and less effective in the world, but faith can certainly survive in that environment. We should also have closely in mind those who might *reject* the faith because of its connection with classics, conservatism or natural law, for ultimately salvation matters more than learning, politics or law and we should never throw out precious babies with more disposable bathwater.

From Mr Heydon's lecture I take the traditional ten ideas of great value and comment very briefly on these possible elements of a new narrative.

Heydon adopts the concept of 'modern elites' to characterize anti-Christian forces. No one in Australia likes elites (or elitism, though they are generally comfortable with elite activities which represent excellence within some form of expertise). Self-appointed elites certainly exist and within the broad family of identity-politics can use the force of their existence as a substitute for detailed and precise argument and fair response to critics. But beneath such modern elites I believe there is a broader, more ground-level hostility to Christianity bred of many elements. These elites sustain and validate this broader base; they do not simply create or cause it. The opposition to Christianity is broad and deep, and the responses required are therefore many and varied.

Heydon also speaks of modern elites aiming to exclude religion generally. This is certainly true and there are various reasons for this, but it is again symptomatic of a broader anti-intellectual platform. Philosophies and worldviews, at their core, give people some insight into fundamental features of reality and of the human condition—discovering how to respond to our situation certainly, but also understanding it, discovering how things really are. This is a great gift of myth in the classical sense: whether religious or not, we have available to us epic accounts of the most important and lasting features of world, person and value. Elites substitute group-interests and the battle for power over attempts to build an understanding of reality and the position and choices we adopt towards it; social moves on power eclipse philosophy's search for meaning and establish no convincing counter-myth. This is a real loss in terms of human insight, the development of wisdom and of our inner lives.

Thirdly, Heydon reminds us that modern elites will not tolerate opposition. No sane person denies the need to think through opposing views and how we might answer them fairly and adequately. Elites are tempted to look for shortcuts. Sometimes this is because people persuade themselves they have the neutral position and thus any opposition represents not a rival view but an outright rejection of what is obvious and normal—a failure to adopt a position at all. This is infuriating, and dangerous of course. People can learn here from Christians at their best—both in their refusal to settle for being a mere power-group and in their willingness to consider respectfully and respond rationally to opposition.

Heydon also makes the excellent point that as the world becomes more comfortable people do not see the need for afterlife and morality. I think this is right. It is deeply irrational. (Even if you believed that comfort and pleasure were what mattered, why would you not at least enquire whether they might continue and even increase?) And the irrationality occurs partly because of what comfort and pleasure feel like while enjoyed—they satiate us, make us lazy, disinclined for effort or the pain of asking, "and afterwards?" In any case, the Four Last Things are rarely visited on a sunny beach. Yet the beach exists at the cost of the battlefield. Death is always around the corner, and its cognates— unhappiness, anxiety, depression, loss, meaninglessness, despair—are also close by. Achievement, friends and distraction through leisure only make sense against mortality and we should all consider it.

When it comes to lack of appetite to think about *morality* this is a major issue demanding a paper in its own right. I fully agree that un-interest in or apathy about morality is more characteristic of our elites than taking a radical or extreme position *within* morality. Kant explored beautifully where our actual interest in morality comes from—an important and underexplored topic. His answer—that from the recognition we are bound by moral law come sentiments of reverence and respect toward that law which sustain our moral interest—is a good one, though there are others (the divine, by which I do not precisely mean religious faith, comes to mind). Core to un-interest in morality is deficiency in how elites understand human persons and societies. Without a concept of what a person really is, and so what is genuinely good for persons (even if not wished for by them), and what is genuinely required of societies, it is hard to be interested in morality as anything other than arbitrary rules or personal preferences. We are far beyond postmodernism today and in a place, morally speaking, we can no longer accurately name.

Fifthly and sixthly, Heydon describes the lack of a serious, intelligent concept of faith in today's elites, noting faith is thought of as just another matter of taste or preference. Further, elites tend to ignore both courtesy and reason. Again, I think this is right. The concept of faith held by non-believers, and many believers, is reduced to preference and placed on a level with other preferences. And this is quite misleading; at least as misleading as saying someone's greatest personal loves are mere preferences on the level of a preference for cottage cheese. Faith is a commitment to divinity and transcendence; it makes claims of the deepest metaphysical nature; it pins us to a position on origins and destiny, human nature and purpose; and it grounds our whole understanding of ethics and choice. This is no mere preference or taste.

Not even to consider such a concept of faith is to miss out on a major part of education, knowledge and culture. It is to suffer real intellectual impoverishment akin to missing out on the major concepts behind politics, physics or economics. And with ignorance of faith will come ignorance of reason: our concept of reason is clarified historically in a debate concerning faith, and a full sense of reason today still positions it with respect to faith, truth-seeking and other key concepts. Faith and reason require each other, and together they give rise to a number of social tendencies, including increased respect, civility and courtesy. Courtesy is both a mode of communicating and an attitude towards others. Courtesy has almost vanished as a moral currency in place of respect, which matters but which is easily portrayed as a sort of wariness of others, keeping our distance and observing boundaries. There is more to respect of course, and courtesy laces that respect with kindness and manners, which are, again, harder to grasp and to promote in a society devoid of concepts of faith or reason.

Heydon argues liberalism came from Christianity. As a matter of logic and history it is hard to see where else liberalism might have come from. Many goods, and of course some bads, have come from Christianity over the centuries. And amongst these is equality, which Christ taught repeatedly throughout the New Testament and St Paul unpacked to the original churches of the Mediterranean world. The idea of anyone else in this period proclaiming this notion with such originality, conviction and consistency is almost laughable.

What can have no public expression will soon have no private existence, states Heydon. This is probably true both psychologically and logically (hermetical private life, language and existence are incoherent concepts and unsustainable realities). More important is the social and moral point: if we are compelled not to express publicly and practically what we ought to be able to express, then all sorts of bad effects result. Internally, we will suffer division and confusion, anxiety, frustration and maybe shame. Socially, we no longer offer witness and share bodily, communal celebration. No religion survives this pressure. Religion of its nature is lived, communicated, handed on, discussed, shared, made incarnate and made visible. Suppression of practice is ultimately coercion of belief—and pressure to unbelieve.

Finally, Heydon notes that some may think that the time for resistance has come. This would always be Christian resistance. For, as mentioned above, there is no point joining an ideological battle and throwing lines (or worse) back in people's faces, even if this seems just and merited. The present narrative is strong and Christians are likely to lose any ideological battle against it. Instead of battle, the right tools are very ancient ones: (final) perseverance in the faith, clear and repeated reasoning over complex matters, kindness and politeness towards those with whom we disagree, forgiveness even in the face of terrible wrongs, tempering our anger, showing prudence over excitability in our communications. This has no guarantee of stopping a spit or a punch, but it is a matter of creed that this is what we do, and no one should ever drive us to do otherwise. Such a narrative seems to me today extraordinarily compelling if dormant and awaiting the words and images of tomorrow's poets, saints, scholars and mystics.

8

A WARNING TO CONSERVATIVE ELITES

Shireen Morris

Dyson Heydon is correct: a persuasive argument should not attempt to conceal the strength of the case against it. Rather, the opposing view should be engaged and addressed. Or better still, the persuader should glean new learning from the opposing case, to modify and improve her own position—to forge, where possible, as yet undiscovered common ground. Wisdom comes not from arguing in echo chambers and dismissing different views—it comes from hearing and understanding those with alternative perspectives and learning something from them.

In his PM Glynn Lecture, Heydon argues that the "tyranny of relativism" and the "tyranny of tolerance" in modern Australia—the rise of political correctness, secularism and the trend of simply shouting down one's opponents—are threatening to undermine important religious and social institutions and the time-honoured values they represent. Heydon critiques the modern culture of political debate as more rancorous than reasoned: key players are unhelpfully prone to offence and too tribal to take on board differing views. Heydon also observes hypocrisy in the contemporary practice of tolerance. The claim is that "modern elites", as Heydon strategically calls them (more on this later), like to insist that everyone must be tolerant, yet they themselves do not tolerate opposing views.

Some of Heydon's observations are valid. Political debate has become tribal. There are echo chambers. People are often unwilling to engage meaningfully with opposing views. Political debate—especially with the rise of social media—is increasingly lacking in reason and rationality.

The weakness in Heydon's argument, however, is that it does not acknowledge the extent to which such faults are demonstrated amongst progressives and conservatives alike. Nor does it acknowledge the grave responsibility conservatives bear in failing to engage with the valid complaints of progressive critics. Heydon sees the flaws in progressive modes of debate but admits none of the flaws in conservative approaches, nor in the conservative orthodoxy he attempts to defend—the demise of which Heydon fears is imminent.

As this essay will show, if the demise of conservative institutions and values is in fact imminent, conservatives themselves must bear primary responsibility. Heydon's argument is therefore narrow in scope and lacks self-reflection. It criticises tribal deafness, but it is itself tribal and deaf to legitimate criticisms of its own position. Heydon has not adequately acknowledged the strength of the progressive case against his argument.

The best thinkers, when dealing with vexing policy, legal and political problems, take on board the legitimate concerns of their opponents, learn from them, and forge a new and better synthesis position. They find the elusive 'radical centre' between competing philosophies. Finding the radical centre requires both parties to shift. This requires humility and intelligence—for the smartest people know they cannot be right on everything, and even their rightness can be refined. The insights of others, bringing different life experiences, can open our minds—if only we have the courage to hear what others say. It also shows empathy. Listening and acknowledging opposing views lets others know their grievances have been heard. Feeling heard is conducive to cohesion, inclusion and unity.

I advocate empathetic debate and discussion across ideological divides. I advocate the intelligent seeking of the radical centre—the noble compromise. I do not advocate moral relativism, much less its tyrannical enforcement. There is a difference. A noble compromise does not force another to yield to their view—at least not completely. It finds the brilliant centre between competing concerns.

Heydon warns against the tyranny of moral relativism and the risk that conservative institutions and values become undermined by attack from the tyrannically tolerant—those "modern elites" who are said to force their version of tolerance on everyone, to the point that the tolerance itself becomes intolerant—that is, it becomes intolerant of what the "modern elites" perceive as intolerance. Modern elites are thus "tyrants of tolerance", Heydon argues. This is the alleged tolerance paradox Heydon so detests.

The most serious problem with Heydon's argument is that it omits any serious discussion of power, and power relationships. In the past, it was those in power forcing their *intolerance* down everyone's throats, often against their will, through laws, policies and government decisions on unjust and discriminatory bases. Racial intolerance was more prevalent.[1] Sexual and gender intolerance was widespread.[2] Religious intolerance, which is Heydon's main concern, was more prevalent too. In the early years of the colony of New South Wales, there were prohibitions on Catholic group observance.[3] There were also policies forbidding the practice of Aboriginal religions, traditions and languages in favour of mandated assimilation in missions (though some missions thankfully helped Aboriginal people record and keep their languages and cultures).[4] And across the world people once killed each other more readily in promotion or defence of their religious creed.

Things changed with the gradual adoption of Enlightenment principles. The Enlightenment saw reason and rationalism overtake religious dogma. Secularism meant increased separation of the church and state. Principles of democracy began to outweigh or at least temper ideas of the born-to-rule aristocracy, and arbitrary discrimination became less acceptable ways to organise society. Liberalism meant the rise of the individual at the expense of the ancient, the spiritual, the communal and the traditional.

The Enlightenment's principles of freedom and equality necessarily entailed increased tolerance for difference. But it took a while for these principles to themselves be applied equally, especially in relation to the dark-skinned among us. Thomas Jefferson drafted America's founding constitutional documents extolling the virtues of liberty and equality, yet as a white man he was a slave-owner, as was the norm of the time. It was not until much later, when Martin Luther King Jnr and other civil rights activists insisted that the constitutional promises of freedom and equality be extended to non-white Americans, that the 'all men are created equal' ethos began to be more fairly realised.

In Australia, there has been a similar progression towards tolerance over time. The illiberal discrimination practiced by the colonisers has been toned down by successive parliaments. There are no longer laws banning homosexual sex and same-sex couples can now marry. Prohibitions on Catholicism are long forgotten. Indigenous Australians now have the vote across jurisdictions and can marry whom they choose—though they are still far from enjoying substantive social and economic parity. The White Australia Policy is gone and we are now, by and large, a successful multicultural democracy. Though there is a constant need for vigilance to guard against a return to less tolerant times, the fact remains that our society and attitudes have significantly changed for the better. Tolerance has won in Australia. This has given rise to a trendy new reactionary complaint: the existential complaint of some conservatives pining for the past.

The worry of some conservatives now—though perhaps they are better described as reactionaries—is that tolerant secular liberals have grown more powerful at the expense of conservative values. Those espousing progressive views have increased in number, and now threaten to democratically overpower the whims of the old intolerant who used to call all the shots. The tolerant may now become the oppressors, is the anxious claim. They will seek to stifle the views and activities of those who used to do the oppressing—by outlawing their intolerant practices, perhaps, or shouting them down in their greater numbers. This is the new PC orthodoxy set to erode our fundamental rights and freedoms—so goes the reactionary argument. Now that progressivism is gathering steam at the expense of conservatism, it is conservatives who increasingly cry, "poor me." This reaction is overblown. It is a form of victimhood. How can it be a bad thing that our society has become more tolerant? It must surely be a good shift from the discrimination and prejudice of the past.

The existential angst and insecurity being experienced by the stalwart defenders of the old white Western Christian dominance, traditions and power structures—eloquently expressed by Heydon in his speech—is ironic in this regard. These are the concerns of a constituency who, in a real sense, is anxious about the impending end of their reign. Their anxiety is understandable: maybe they know and remember how they treated those at the bottom, when they were on top. Now that the tables may be turning, will their 'white rights' be squashed with equal disdain and nonchalance? Will they be told they cannot practice their religion and culture, in the same way some of their forebears forbade Aborigines, for example?

The anxiety Heydon expresses may be ironic, but it is important progressives hear conservative concerns, and vice versa. Wrongdoing is not justified just because someone else did wrong before. It is important all Australians are free to practice their religions and traditions, so long as this practice does not infringe on the rights of others. This is fundamental to a free and democratic nation.

A moral society must strike the right balance between competing rights and freedoms. This requires communication and negotiation across ideological divides and party lines. Across interest groups, ethnicities and class. Across left and right. It requires the parties to hear each other's anxieties, negotiate, and find the noble compromise. The problem is not the increase in tolerance. That is a good thing. The problem arises when the appropriate balance is not struck: when just tolerance grows at the expense of certain other freedoms, or at the expense of valued traditions and institutions—or more accurately—at the expense of the *good parts* of those traditions and institutions.

If the devaluing of tradition is a reality, conservatives must bear responsibility. Many conservatives have for too long lacked compassion and empathy. Instead of listening and negotiating with progressives in good faith, they opt for deafness, dismissal and obstinance to change. This does not lead to victory for their conservative cause. Rather, they end up losing key debates to progressives, who increasingly have the numbers.

I heed Heydon's warning on the tyranny of tolerance, and can understand the existential anxiety he and others are expressing. But to Heydon and his conservative constituency I offer this reciprocal warning: if conservative elites (to use a Heydon-esque generalisation) do not find ways to hear, understand, and adapt to the genuine concerns of those their institutions and power structures for so long excluded and oppressed, they risk undermining the very traditions, institutions and values they seek to protect.

Institutions suffering obstinate sclerosis are prone to breakage. Structures that bend and evolve flexibly have longevity—for they are responsive to the desires and needs of the people. True conservatives know that evolution is part of life. The trouble is, modern conservative elites are usually more inclined to complain about and dismiss their ideological combatants than acknowledge the strength of opposing arguments and adjust accordingly.

Instead, debate oscillates at the extreme fringes and sensible progress is forsaken. Reasoned discourse gives way to tribal point-scoring and name-calling. Sensible and innovative solutions slip through the cracks, in favour of reactionary polemic. It is not just the left that is guilty of such tribalism. The right is equally guilty. Each side too often fails to grapple with the rational concerns of the other.

Heydon attacks the vanity and hypocrisy of what he calls the "modern elites". As becomes immediately clear in the lecture, the term is a strategic euphemism for "progressive elites". One can elucidate what Heydon means by "modern elites" from his comparison with what he calls "Federation generation" elites—but which I will call the "colonial elites"—the founding fathers who convened to create the Australian Constitution. He notes they drafted a constitutional preamble which included the words "humbly relying on the blessing of Almighty God".

These words, Heydon argues, "reflected what the elite of the Federation generation saw as fundamental": principles of humility, gratitude, and the belief in a higher power. Heydon draws a distinction between the humble and grateful attitudes of the colonial elites in 1900, and the entitled and demanding voices of the modern progressive elites in 2018. "The public voices of modern elites are not humble," Heydon states, "They conceive themselves to have entitlements and rights, not blessings. And they do not feel any gratitude to Almighty God for their entitlements and rights."

But what made the colonial elites, elites? In my view, one thing alone: power. Military colonial power. And thus, political, legal and financial power. Their white skins, too, in line with the colonial politics and ethos of the era. They were the conquerors. They were indeed elites, in every sense of the term.

The colonial elites were running the show, in a situation where British sovereignty had been declared and asserted to the detriment of the First Nations who had owned the land for thousands of years prior. The British asserted control and possession, dispossessing the original Indigenous owners. They then negotiated between themselves the terms by which their disparate colonies would unite as an indissoluble Commonwealth, and included no Indigenous representatives in these discussions. The power-sharing agreement forged—the Australian Constitution—contained clauses specifically excluding Indigenous people and presided over decades of discriminatory laws and policies about them.[5]

I can therefore understand why the colonial elites counted their blessings. They had every reason to thank God. Some believed themselves, according to evidence in the Constitutional Convention debates, to be superior to their inferior dark-skinned counterparts.[6] Such superiority, often believed to be related to Christianity and religious justifications, along with commercial and political justifications, was used in favour of colonial conquest (though religious arguments were also used against it).[7] The doctrine of discovery, under international law of the colonial era, held that usurpation of foreign nations was allowed where those nations were not ruled by a Christian monarch—a convenient rule. The Eurocentric view saw Christian societies as more civilized and enlightened, and native non-white societies as heathen and barbarian, without recognisable laws or ownership of land.[8] Such attitudes worked to justify Indigenous dispossession by colonial powers.

The colonial elites asserted dominance over a vast new continent.

They had much to be grateful for. Correspondingly, the Indigenous peoples who suffered decades of dispossession, discrimination and violence at the hands of the conquerors, had much to be angry and sad about. They lost out so a great nation could rise up on an ancient continent. They are still losing out today.

Indigenous people also carry a conservative existential angst. It is an anxiety, as Noel Pearson has described, that they, their peoples, traditions and cultures, will be wiped from the face of the earth—eradicated by the forces of the more powerful colonial elites who asserted dominance in 1788 and in 1901 and still retain this structural dominance. The colonial elites did not hear the existential cry of the First Nations, though it came time and again—through petitions, letters to the King, and now through the historic Uluru Statement from the Heart. The colonial elites were deaf to it. So too, often, are the modern conservative elites.

The colonial elites Heydon describes with nostalgic reverence can therefore be distinguished from the contemporary progressive interest groups Heydon dismisses as "modern elites", because the colonial elites possessed real power. In their constitutional compact, they authoritatively decided how power was to be shared out in the new nation. They gave themselves all the power and gave Indigenous people none. Those power structures persist today. This is the point.

The progressive modern elites Heydon talks about with palpable disdain, tend to advocate the rights of the *powerless*. They seek recognition of the rights of the disempowered. These progressives seek constitutional, institutional and structural reform to share power and resources more equitably, so that groups who suffered injustice, exclusion and oppression in the past and present—like Indigenous peoples for example—might be given a fairer go in the future. But the defenders of the status quo—the moral guardians of the Constitution, of tradition, of Australia's British institutional inheritance—usually do not even hear them out, let alone address their concerns through efforts at constitutional and institutional reform.

Notice how Heydon's term 'elite' seeks to frame the group in question as an out-of-touch minority? The same-sex marriage plebiscite demonstrated that this kind of terminology is misleading and false. Tony Abbott must now have to admit that the "silent majority" of "ordinary Australians" that he claimed his anti-same-sex marriage stance represented, is actually a minority: 75 per cent of Abbott's electorate voted 'yes' to same-sex marriage. It was the majority of Australians who found a voice in that debate. The Liberal Party insisted on the postal survey. But Abbott did not respect the survey's outcome. He left the parliamentary chamber before the final vote on the legislation, along with his conservative colleague, Michael Sukkar, who previously promised he would respect his electorate's wishes.[9] Sukkar's electorate, Deakin, voted 65.7 per cent in favour of same sex marriage—above the national average—but Sukkar ran out of the parliamentary chamber behind Abbott when the final vote was imminent.

What does this say about how connected the conservative elite are to the ordinary Australians? Is it any wonder there is frustration amongst their progressive opponents and the people they are supposed to represent? It was not the "modern elites" pushing same-sex marriage. This is Heydon's unsuccessful attempt at flipping the table: framing his conservative constituency as the underdog, the silenced majority (who are really a noisy minority), the victims.

Modern conservative elites are not victims—but they are understandably nervous about the change happening around them. And Heydon's "modern elites" are, in fact, not elites—they are ordinary, progressive, empathetic Australians, who see the injustice of the past and present and want change for the better. The conservative elites are the defenders of the old Australia—and they are losing. They are running out of the chamber, deaf to the legitimate wishes of the majority.

The obstinance of the conservative elite gives rise to a fractious, impolite impasse. There is impatience, anger and rancour amongst progressives who want change, and growing progressive disillusionment in our national institutions that have for so long been deaf to legitimate Indigenous and other concerns. It also gives rise to rage and uncouth language, particularly amongst young activists. This understandably hurts the already fragile ears of the contemporary conservative elite—

further defeating any chance at coherent conversation across ideological divides.

Indigenous activist Tarneen Onus-Williams declared at an 'invasion day' rally this year that "Australia should burn to the ground". This was an inappropriate and strategically unwise comment (and Onus-Williams was quick to clarify that her comment should not be taken literally). I do not agree that Australia should burn to the ground, obviously—Heydon says it is important I make this clear, lest people assume I condone the burning scenario—but I understand where the anger and impatience comes from.

The conservative elites were quick to jump on Onus-Williams for her remark. Yet one may also ask: what have the conservative elite done to instigate sensible structural change that might address legitimate Indigenous concerns? The answer is: little. Conservative elites have often ignored, derided or rejected many more sensible proposals for reform. Proposals that involve no burning of any kind have been callously dismissed—including proposals that would uphold and strengthen the Australian Constitution and its institutions, rather than incinerate them.

Look at the cruel and parsimonious way the Uluru Statement's call for a constitutionally entrenched Indigenous advisory body was rejected by the political right. This was a rare radical-centre proposal designed by Indigenous activists in concert with constitutional conservatives. The upholders collaborated with the reformers to devise a modest yet profound proposal. Yet the contemporary conservative elites—with some notable exceptions, to be fair—mostly either refused to engage with this sensible proposed reform or rejected it outright. Then they complain about fiery young activists who have understandably become impatient for justice.

When conservatives ignore sensible calls for reform, the ferocity and urgency of discontent grows ever greater, and the authority and popularity of conservative institutions diminish over time. This conservative head-in-the-sand strategy is unwise: they are losing the battle of public opinion with respect to the traditions and institutions they hold most dear. More Australians now march in the Invasion Day parade in Melbourne, than the Australia Day parade. What does this tell us about how well conservative elites are doing at responding to legitimate Indigenous concerns, and legitimate public concerns, about the need for proper reconciliation, recognition and reform?

"But there is more wrong with the approach of the elites than discourtesy," Heydon argues, "Their approach disables them from— makes them incapable of—presenting their point of view, for what it is worth, properly. To shout is not to argue. To censor is not to reason. To bawl is not to engage in persuasion." Thus, Heydon bemoans the loss of "courtesy, civility and mutual respect" in contemporary debates. I agree, but both sides demonstrate discourtesy. The more important question is: which will be the first to rise above their acrimony and lead a better way forward for the country? "You're racist. Burn," says one. "You're impolite. I will dismiss you as a 'modern elite' and, when I'm out-numbered, I will run out of the parliamentary chamber," says the other. How do these polar forces meet in the middle, if this is the intelligence of the debate?

The challenge with communication across ideological divides is not just to hear what people are saying when they say it in ways we approve of: the challenge is to understand the concerns of people and constituencies who experience, think, feel and speak in ways we may find different, abrasive, offensive and challenging, and to get to the bottom of their concerns nonetheless—if at all possible. To become focussed on rambunctious or impolite language is to miss the deeper complaint which may be valid.

Heydon's call for courtesy is actually just a call for political correctness, this time pushed by the right. It's one thing to complain about an opponent's language and style. But where is the engagement with the substance of opposing arguments? Where is the engagement at the sensible centre?

Australia Day tensions will persist, and should persist, until our nation comes to terms with the wrongs of the past and resolves them through formal reconciliation. For this to happen, conservative elites must engage with legitimate Indigenous concerns.[10] Achieving such a resolution requires courageous moral leadership on both sides. It requires us to rise above our tribalism and come together for the national good. It requires us to respect the ancient and the old properly, and embrace the new, to bring these things together to create a fuller conception of who we are as Australians.

Paul Kelly wrote in *The Australian* on current Australian conservatism:

> Where are its leaders? Where is its moral force? What happened to its institutional authority? Conservatives these days excel at drum-beating, making a lot of noise, writing a lot of articles and losing every substantial battle. They are fragmented, intellectually confused and strategically inept. Much of the nation is still conservative in its instincts but this constituency is denied inspiring or effective leadership.[11]

Noel Pearson followed up powerfully:

> Kelly is right that conservatism is on the backfoot. My argument is conservative leaders and their followers have themselves to blame for their predicaments. They have set up their own reversals.
>
> They have done this by failing to maintain the distinction between genuine conservatism and bigotry and prejudice. There is such a thing as compassionate conservatism, but it has been overshadowed by a meanness in public conservatism, as if intolerance and offence-giving is a mark of courage and principle. . . .
>
> . . . conservatism in Australia . . . has developed a virulent form of obscurantism among its followers: head in the sand, impervious to reason, and a relentless certitude in the correctness of their view. A pestilent irrationality has taken hold of conservative discourse in this country that is highly ideological and resistant to science and reason. Just because the leftists have their own stupidities does not excuse this practice.[12]

Pearson is correct: it is the conservative elite's failure to grapple properly with the public popularity of many significant social justice issues that has resulted in the decline of conservative values and institutions. The popularity of same-sex marriage, and the refusal of the conservative elite to whole-heartedly engage with this, has given rise to Kelly's worry that religious freedom is not appropriately protected. Arguably, conservatives had many chances to engage in a genuine search for the noble compromise on this issue and many others. There is a lesson here for the conservative elite.

I was astounded to watch staunch right-wing opponents of a bill of rights change their tunes during the same-sex marriage debate—as soon as their own rights to religious freedom were at stake. Suddenly members of the conservative elite, like Paul Kelly, were quoting from United Nations human rights treaties and urging legislation to protect religious freedom rights. Why? Because conservative elites are worried, as Heydon explains, that "the tyrants of tolerance" will "pay lip-service, but only lip-service, to freedom of religion as a fundamental human right." Suddenly we see conservatives arguing for stronger legislated rights protection—a quasi-bill of rights. Because, evidently, empowering unelected judges is acceptable when the rights of the privileged are at stake.

Conservative elites ferociously opposed any legislated bill of rights in the past, because they didn't want to empower the High Court. They opposed the Expert Panel's attempt to insert a racial non-discrimination guarantee in the Constitution, for the same reason. But now that they are worried about their own rights—suddenly their United Nations-declared human rights should be legislatively protected?

The self-serving nature of such position-shifting is obvious. The conservative elite oppose rights protection, except when their own constituency's rights are at stake. There is zero empathy for the valid concerns of others.

"If section 18C is to stay, why is religion not given the protection it affords?" Heydon asks. Ignoring the fact that religious freedom is partly protected by the Constitution, whereas the Constitution explicitly allows racial discrimination (as Heydon's own judgements have confirmed), Australia's rights protection is haphazard and uneven precisely because the conservative elite have historically preferred this. The colonial elite did not want a bill of rights—they preferred the common law and the checks and balances of federalism. The contemporary conservative elite did not want a federal bill of rights either.

Lacking a bill of rights, Australia's rights protections have developed sporadically, under common law and legislation, depending on the politics and trends of the day. This was how conservatives wanted it. This has resulted is a system that protects rights through legislation and focusses on discrimination, rather than positive declared protections of rights.

Heydon, evidently experiencing a form of postcolonial victim-envy, complains that "real tolerance extends only to those who are alleged to be victims of discrimination." Yet I struggle to feel sorry for conservative elites who now want better legislative protection of their religious freedom, when those same conservative elites virulently opposed constitutional racial non-discrimination protection when Indigenous people (understandably, given the history) requested it in 2012; and who wanted to water down section 18C of the Racial Discrimination Act to make it easier to racially vilify black people in 2014; and who now refuse to allocate Indigenous peoples the right even to a non-binding voice when Parliament makes decisions about their specific rights.

I equally struggle to feel sorry for churches who for a long time handled allegations of child abuse poorly, with cover ups and unwillingness to pay just compensation to victims, and who also took the moral high ground in refusing gay couples inclusion into the institution of marriage. Heydon decries the foolishness of activists who argued we should "burn churches, not gays". I agree that such illiberal statements are unacceptable, but is not compassionate inclusion the best—and indeed the most Christian—antidote to such frustrated sentiment? The Catholic Church should have sat down with gay activists long ago to figure out a way of addressing their legitimate desire to be treated equally by being included in the institution of marriage, while upholding religious freedom.

This is what Noel Pearson and I did in devising a proposal for a constitutionally enshrined Indigenous body to advise Parliament: we sat down with compassionate conservatives and forged common ground. But the radical centre compromise we forged, subsequently endorsed at Uluru, was rejected by an incompetent political leadership in the Liberal Party in October 2017. They chose not to bend—then people are surprised by more radical suggestions that the Constitution should burn.

The call by excluded groups for inclusion and recognition within an institution, like the Indigenous call for inclusion in the Australian Constitution, or the call by gay people for inclusion within the institution of marriage, is a compliment to those institutions. It shows respect. It shows a desire to be included, to unite, to end the conflict. When the conservative elite respond to such requests with scorn and rejection, "burn churches" and "burn Australia" is the unintelligent result. The discourse becomes relegated to the reactionary fringes. The sensible centre remains unexplored and unrealised. Conservatism leaves itself open to this kind of unnuanced attack by progressives, because it does not adopt nuanced and sensible approaches to reform when the opportunity is there.

The conservative elite are now experiencing a small taste of the existential anxiety Indigenous people have experienced unabated since 1788. The Indigenous anxiety too is conservative in nature—as Noel Pearson described, they fear they will lose their ancient culture, traditions and languages. They fear they will be crushed out of existence by the continued weight of the colonising state, that has always been intolerant of Indigenous expressions of difference and requests for inclusion despite that difference. Now the conservative elite worry the progressive elite might be intolerant of *their* expressions of difference.

If they had compassion, the conservative elite would sit down with Indigenous peoples, as the colonial elite should have done before 1901, talk about their differences and seek common ground. Though we cannot address the concerns of racists—just as we cannot address calls for institutions to burn—there are ways forward that can address the rational concerns of all sensible stakeholders, if they are willing to come to the table with open minds and hearts, and with empathy.

It is possible to recognise Indigenous peoples meaningfully and uphold the Constitution. It is possible to end discrimination against gay people and respect important religious freedoms and institutions. It is possible for us to be tolerant and inclusive of different identities and tolerant and inclusive of different points of view.

What a great country this might be if we did politics in this way.

9

THE MODERN ELITES

Michael Ondaatje

In his PM Glynn Lecture, Dyson Heydon takes aim at "modern elites" for their illiberal attitudes and activities in the context of the nation's culture wars. He pays special attention to these elites' attacks on religion, particularly Christianity, but goes further, accusing them of trying to marginalise or silence *any* views that conflict with their own. For Heydon, modern elites in Australia are the enemies of viewpoint diversity: they prefer to "shout", "censor" and "bawl" while demanding "unconditional surrender" and "absolute victory" for a "dogma which is unchallengeable". But who exactly are these elites? Heydon doesn't specifically identify those whom he is indicting, but by implication their identity is political rather than social. The epithet "elites" needs to be teased out and understood in a wider context, because contemporary anti-elite sentiment is not a peculiarly Australian phenomenon.

As a historian focused on American politics, I can see parallels between what Heydon is describing in Australia and current trends in the United States, at universities, in politics and the media. Today, talk of "microaggressions", "privilege", "trigger warnings" and "safe spaces" is common on American college campuses, as is the phenomenon of "no-platforming", the left-wing tactic of shutting down—or shouting down—conservative or liberal speakers deemed offensive or illegitimate. Such intolerance also manifests in the daily rough and tumble of American politics. Who could forget Hillary Clinton's description of Trump's supporters as "deplorables" in the 2016 presidential election— "racist, sexist, homophobic, xenophobic, Islamaphobic"? And what of the media? Just as universities have "diversity tsars" to police thought and enforce orthodoxy, the *New York Times* now has a "gender editor" committed to introducing an "intersectional" approach—blending race, class and gender analyses—in every section of the newspaper. Although Heydon's focus is Australia, I suspect these are the "modern elites" he has in mind: academics, politicians and journalists who are obsessed with "identity", out of touch with ordinary people and who, in Sarah Palin's words, think "that they're better than anyone else".

If my assessment is correct, then I am somewhat sympathetic to Heydon's negative portrayal of "modern elites". The liberal ideal of free speech is precious and must be defended against those on campus who would quash it in the name of "justice" for the oppressed. Moreover, elite condescension is rarely productive or justified. Not only is it bad politics (again, think Hillary Clinton), it also reflects a disturbing "empathy deficit" towards people holding different views from one's own. To be sure, this kind of condescension is evident across the political spectrum, from tribal left to tribal right. Now more than ever, it seems, liberal democracy needs a common civic language that speaks to people collectively and as individuals, and that promotes a robust diversity of opinion without regard to political correctness and fragile sensitivities. For reason to prevail, an open marketplace of ideas is essential. Dyson Heydon laments the absence of such a marketplace in Australia, particularly in discussions of religion, and lays the blame squarely at the feet of "modern elites".

One senses that Heydon's elites are defined by culture rather than class, and by their political commitments rather than how much money they have in the bank. In Australia, they are likely to live in the inner city, read *The Saturday Paper*, eat tofu and vote Green (or Labor), while sneering at fellow citizens who might be anxious about immigration, opposed to gay marriage, and critical of Safe Schools. Calling out condescending, 'know-it-all' elites can be enough to establish you as a 'voice of the people' in most liberal democracies today. Look no further than the 2016 presidential election in the United States. As well as relentlessly attacking the 'elite' liberal media, Donald Trump used Hillary Clinton's political experience against her, portraying the former First Lady and Secretary of State as a crooked Washington 'insider' hopelessly out-of-touch with ordinary people. The fact that Trump was a billionaire Ivy League graduate who had inherited significant wealth and lived in a gold tower seemed irrelevant to those who hated 'elites' and voted *for* him accordingly. Brexit revealed similar political dynamics in the United Kingdom. 'Leave' activists slammed 'liberal elites' for opposing their campaign, but the face of the campaign was Boris Johnson, an Eton-and-Oxford-educated Tory who could hardly be considered one of that nation's 'ordinary people'.

Whilst I concur with much in Heydon's essay—in particular, his key point that political correctness inhibits rational discussion and is toxic for politics—I question the choice of the term "elites" to frame the analysis, and the value of the term, as it is currently employed in politics more broadly. Today, it seems that everyone is railing against 'elites' in one form or other—liberal elites, ruling elites, secular elites, business elites, bureaucratic elites, cultural elites, economic elites, urban elites, educated elites, the list goes on. The term is used by very different people to attack wildly different targets, but usually with a common purpose—to call out opponents for having 'undeserved privileges' and preventing 'honest' people from getting a fair deal. The word has evolved significantly since sociologist C. Wright Mills used it in the 1950s to describe a class of people that held direct political and economic power, irrespective of party affiliation (Republican or Democrat, Liberal or Labor) or consumer tastes (red meat or tofu). Now, anyone in a position of influence, that someone else thinks they do not deserve, is in danger of being labelled and dismissed as an 'elite'. Such is the nature of life in modern liberal democracies.

The current anger at 'elites' is hardly surprising. In 2007, elite financiers are believed to have 'stuffed' the global economy, deepening long-term trends towards inequality, while political elites are thought to have responded ineffectively to the crisis. Today, we are more attuned to historical injustices against minorities and the benefits of diversity, but we treat 'whiteness' as a problem to be overcome and the economic plight of poor whites as an afterthought. Increasingly, these people feel demonised culturally, isolated socially and ignored economically— rebuked for their identity, values and faith, with fewer avenues for socialisation as communities break down, and diminishing opportunity to make a decent living in the global economy. These problems are particularly acute in the United States and Britain, but we are kidding ourselves if we think we are immune from these issues—and the resulting disaffection—in Australia. In recent years, public trust and confidence in Australian democracy have dropped to record lows, and voters have expressed serious dissatisfaction with the major parties and the 'political class'.

To be sure, Dyson Heydon's essay was not about this bigger political picture, but it did address a critical—and related—issue within modern Australian politics: how the role of religion is understood by 'elites' in an increasingly secular and complex liberal democracy. Heydon might have titled his essay "the new intolerance". His thesis is that elites— very broadly defined—do not understand or, more accurately, *do not wish to understand*, religious faith and the religious contribution in Australian society. These people distort religion and then condemn it with little regard for nuance, all the while professing their commitment to tolerance and diversity. There is some truth to Heydon's charge. I am hardly an expert on religion but as a humanities scholar I have been around enough university conversations to know the low esteem in which Christianity, in particular, is held in some academic circles. As an historian, I am also aware of the extent to which religion has been 'written out' of Australian history—the subject is rarely taught in history departments and it is not exactly a growth area in research. It is perhaps not surprising, then, that there is so little religious literacy around us, even though the majority of Australians have always identified—and still identify—as Christians.

To the extent that Heydon calls out "intolerance" towards Christianity and Christians in modern Australia, I am with him. There was an abundance of this intolerance in the recent marriage equality debate, although, to be fair, the mean-spiritedness often ran both ways. In her recent book, *Strangers in Their Own Land*, American sociologist Arlie Hochschild challenged readers to climb the "empathy wall" to try and understand where Trump supporters are coming from, rather than simply condemning them as bigots, misogynists, racists and homophobes. My old friend and mentor, the late John Hirst, would have heartily approved. Hirst preferred 'History as explanation' to 'History as advocacy', believing that the best scholars—and indeed the best citizens—were those who learned to deal fairly with what they instinctively disliked. In an era where political invective and name-calling has trumped rational analysis and respectful debate, it is incumbent upon all of us to resist the easy stereotypes and slogans to which we have grown accustomed and to be better citizens—engaging those with whom we disagree, seeking to understand their views and ultimately making a coherent and compelling case for why they should change their mind. Wouldn't the sight of Dyson Heydon breaking bread or tofu with one of his "elites", climbing the empathy wall together, be one to behold—a classical example of democracy in action? After all, what is the alternative?

10

RELATIVISM, TOLERANCE AND MORALITY

Sandra Lynch

In his inaugural PM Glynn lecture, Dyson Heydon, quotes from Larry Siedentop who argues that "the atmosphere of the New Testament is one of exhilarating detachment from the unthinking constraints of inherited social rules".[1] The reference to the unthinking constraints of inherited social rules alerts the reader to a concern about the possibility of thoughtless, short-sighted, parochial, and perhaps intolerant social rules or norms. Heydon supports Siedentop's defence of the cultural tradition of Christianity, which he presents as a prefiguration of modern liberalism; one that "endeavoured to create governmental structures which protected the private sphere of individual freedom", a sphere in which religious belief could survive. The emphasis on free choice is notable and is reflected in the counter-cultural impetus of Christianity, which directs its followers to recognise that all human beings are both equal before God and free to accept the gift of grace attained through faith in Christ. This emphasis on freedom to accept and practice one's faith is juxtaposed in Heydon's lecture to a concern with religious intolerance and discrimination in contemporary Australia.

At the same time, Heydon challenges a notion of tolerance that he argues has become its own form of intolerance, arguing that contemporary "tyrants of tolerance" seek to marginalise or silence the views of Christians. It is not clear whether Heydon has in mind particular views grounded in the faith commitments of Christians or a more general claim. However, questions of the nature of tolerance, its relationship to intolerance, its justifications and its limits are complex. They suggest that we must consider what tolerance implies and whether being tolerant presumes that we must be relativists about values, beliefs and practices. If we are pushed in this direction, what does this mean for attempts to

121

adjudicate between values, beliefs and practices when they come into conflict or cause conflict? If we reject being defined as relativists, how are we to understand the concept of tolerance? If we are not prepared to tolerate what we find objectionable, how do we answer reasonable others who ask us to justify our intolerance? This essay attempts to address these questions, as well as the underlying question of the nature of our commitment to moral values, in three sections. The first section begins with an exploration of the concept of tolerance and consideration of scepticism about the role of religiously informed argument in public and political debate on social issues. The second section focuses on the relationship between tolerance and relativism. The concluding section explores factors that are likely to contribute positively to debate on moral disagreement and to the protection of religious freedom in the Australian public square.

The word *tolerance* has its etymological roots in the Latin *tolerare*, which means to put up with, to countenance or to suffer. Rainer Forst notes that it generally refers to the conditional acceptance of, or non-interference with, beliefs, actions or practices that a person considers to be wrong, but recognises as not prohibited or constrained.[2] Thus these are beliefs, actions and practices that one finds objectionable, but is prepared to put up with. We might ask both, why an agent might find them wrong or objectionable and why the agent might be prepared to put up with them. Forst offers some response to these questions, stipulating that the agent must have good reasons for the objection; it cannot simply be a matter of prejudice, bias or hatred. The agent must also have well-justified and non-arbitrary reasons for voluntarily putting up with the objectionable belief or practice.

This makes tolerance more robust than George Washington, and the philosophical architects of the Anglo-American legal tradition, imagined it. Martha Nussbaum argues that these founding fathers saw that reasonable limits must be imposed on what people do in the name of religion when peace and safety and the equal rights of others are at stake. But they wanted limits that were still compatible with a respect for equal liberty and they took toleration to be too 'thin' a concept to do this work.

As President George Washington put it, in writing to the Hebrew Congregation at Newport in August, 1790:

> The citizens of the United States of America have a right to applaud themselves for having given to mankind examples of an enlarged and liberal policy: a policy worthy of imitation. All possess alike liberty of conscience and immunities of citizenship. *It is now no more that toleration is spoken of, as if it was by the indulgence of one class of people, that another enjoyed the exercise of their inherent natural rights.* For happily, the Government of the United States, which gives to bigotry no sanction, to persecution no assistance requires only that they who live under its protection should demean themselves as good citizens, in giving it on all occasions their effectual support.[3]

As Nussbaum notes, Washington associates toleration with the social hierarchy of the Old World, which the founding fathers of the New World wanted to avoid: a hierarchy in which a privileged group indulges the less privileged, but retains the power not to do so, should it change its mind. By contrast, Forst's stipulation that toleration requires us to put up with the objectionable belief or practice voluntarily, such that even if we had the power to prohibit it we would not do so, bolsters or helps 'thicken' toleration as a concept.[4] But a question remains as to whether the concept of toleration can, on its own, provide the grounds to support robust commitment to freedom of religion in a way that is consistent with the political and legal traditions of a liberal democracy. Certainly, it seems that toleration cannot be regarded as a thick concept unless it fulfils a set of accompanying conditions. In fact, Forst argues that "in itself . . . toleration is not a virtue or value; it can only be a value if backed by the right normative reasons".[5] This is not unlike the stipulations that apply to considering courage as a virtue, since we need to know the reasoning motivating an action if we are to regard it as courageous; we will want to know what the danger consists in, what is being risked and for what purpose, if we are to distinguish a courageous action from the bravado of the reckless thief. Similarly with tolerance, we need to be able to distinguish it from bigotry, persecution and hatred.

So what are the well-justified and non-arbitrary reasons for putting up with the expression of religious beliefs and their application in practice? If these can be articulated, both at the philosophical and the practical level, we should be able to conclude that those who are intolerant of such expression and practice are not well-justified in their rejection of the expression of religious beliefs in political debate or in the application of those beliefs in practice, e.g. in the provision of religious education classes in state schools.

In attempting to answer this question, we must recognise that, both within and outside the academy, there is scepticism about the usefulness of religion as a tool for political analysis and debate. Some scholars view religion as a form of camouflage for the promotion of political or economic agendas and hence attempt to unmask it. As Marion Maddox explains, these scholars attempt to make visible what they see as "the power distributions, economic transactions, gender assumptions, environmental devastations and so on which the term [religion] is inclined to privatise, sacralise and therefore protect from critical analysis"; in particular Maddox draws attention to Arnal and McCutcheon's view that "religion is 'first and foremost a political category' [and] . . . its deployment as a category advances some political agendas, and obscures others".[6]

Both within and outside the academy, the secularisation thesis de-veloped during the nineteenth century popularised the prediction that the role of religion in society would diminish under the influence of the rationalist metaphysics of the Enlightenment, with increasing industri-alisation, and the development of science. It was proposed that seculari-sation correlated with increasing existential security, with "the feeling that survival is secure enough that it can be taken for granted".[7] While the secularisation thesis has come under increasing criticism over recent decades,[8] it nonetheless raises questions about the role and influence of religion in social life to which religious believers ought to ensure they can respond. It behoves those wishing to encourage tolerance and pres-ervation of a space for religiously informed argument in political debate to ensure that they clearly articulate their understandings of both the truth and significance of religion in the lives of believers, as well as in public debate and civic life generally.[9]

In his inaugural lecture as Professor of Law at the Institute of Legal Studies at Australian Catholic University in 2005, Frank Brennan noted that given "that we live in a very secular environment, it is sensible for the religious person to put in the work making their case comprehensible and appealing to the nonreligious person".[10] Brennan reflected on the complexity of this kind of task from his own professional experience. Having been labelled a "meddling priest" some years earlier by the then Prime Minister, Paul Keating, Brennan recognised the difficulty of responsibly mixing law, religion and politics; and in particular, his fraught position as a "church person who was not an Aborigine, a miner or a pastoralist" commenting on the High Court's Wik decision (which dealt with the question of the extinction of native title rights in Queensland).[11]

Brennan's lecture canvassed the relevance of religious belief—for citizens or public officials—when it comes to participating in civic life and contributing to the development of law and policy; as well as the appropriate role for religious authorities participating in those processes. He concluded that the primacy of conscience must be the guiding principle, but noted that right judgement, prudence and political savvy all have their place. However, he considered that place to be fraught due to a number of factors; these include public mistrust of church statements, demands for compromise in politics, the utilitarian political calculus that justifies politicians in doing some evil in order to achieve a greater public good, as well as politicians' lack of expertise or specialist knowledge and their sensitivities in relation to confidentiality. Brennan provides both philosophical and practical direction to those attempting to prosecute religiously informed argument in the public square.[12]

The foundation of his argument is recognition of the primacy of conscience, presumably given the condition that conscientious commitments are well-formed or well-justified. We might argue that recognition of respect for the role of conscience in decision-making is important to living an autonomous and fulfilled life—from a religious or a non-religious perspective; and consequently that it ought to be acknowledged as worthwhile within public debate in a liberal democracy, but given the association between conscience and religious faith, this argument is likely to be open to claims of circularity.

However, there is agreement about the fundamental features of just liberal democracies, such as commitment to the freedom and equality of citizens and to the fairness of terms of social cooperation.[13] Robert Audi argues that it is clear that a liberal democracy must respect the autonomy and political rights of persons, including the right to religious freedom; he acknowledges that "religious freedom . . . may be limited in some ways by a morally well-grounded and liberal democracy that is appropriately neutral in matters of religion", but he notes that this point is probably uncontroversial.[14]

His solution to the opposition between what he calls the principle of secular rationale appropriate to a liberal democracy, and the principle of religious rationale is to favour the former, which states that "in liberal democracies, citizens have a prima facie obligation not to advocate or support any law or public policy that restricts human conduct, unless they have, and are willing to offer, adequate secular reason for this advocacy or support".[15] The implication here is that tolerance makes different demands of the believer by comparison with the non-believer. What is ruled out for the believer is "taking religiously grounded reasons as a basis of coercion or other limitations of liberty without adequate independent support from adequate reason grounded . . . in secular considerations".[16]

The demands of tolerance for the non-believer require a suspension of scepticism and a recognition that fellow citizens who are religious have criteria of religious acceptability that are internal to their religion, which guide their decision-making and action, and which are protected by the political right to religious freedom within a liberal democracy. At the same time, the believer must recognise that religious criteria of acceptability that guide their decision-making and their actions may or may not be objectively adequate to their fellow citizens.

This conclusion about the differing demands placed on believers by comparison with non-believers might suggest that a commitment to moral relativism would solve the difficulty of dealing with beliefs, values and practices that we find objectionable, for well-justified reasons, but which are not constrained or prohibited within the society in which we live. The second section of this essay explores this suggestion and the question of the relationship between tolerance and relativism.

Moral relativism is a concept that has a long history and we can turn to Plato for some guidance on this topic. In his dialogue, the *Euthyphro,* Plato has Socrates ask Euthyphro whether the pious or morally right thing is beloved by the gods because it is right, or right because it is beloved by the gods (or in more common parlance, whether a thing is good because the gods command it or whether the gods command it because it is good). The former possibility has a contemporary and secular analogue in questions related to the validity of moral relativism. Are beliefs or practices right because individuals or cultural groups who hold those views say they are and uphold them; or are they right independently of the views of any particular individual or group? The meta-ethical question here is one that asks whether truth in moral matters and our capacity to justify our moral beliefs is culturally and historically contingent or not. The increasing awareness of cultural diversity among people and of the variety of different ways of living, both secular and religious, gives this question more significance. But as David Wong points out,[17] this question is not a descriptive one, in that it is not a question of whether cultural norms or customs do in fact influence what individuals or groups think is right; clearly they do. Rather it is a philosophical question that asks whether cultural norms actually determine what is right or wrong. The concomitant normative questions ask whether we are right to judge or criticise those who have beliefs that differ from our own and which we find objectionable or even whether we are right to criticise their beliefs, on the grounds that they differ from our own and we find them objectionable.

As C. A. J. Coady explains, one of the least attractive but nonetheless influential forms of moral relativism, what he calls simple cultural relativism, suggests that the only route to tolerance is by denial of the validity of any cross-cultural and supra-cultural (non-relativistic) moral judgements.[18] Coady recognises that there are more sophisticated treatments of relativism offered in the literature and he specifically mentions Simon Blackburn's argument that there are legitimate ways of criticising at least some of the moral views of other cultures, but Coady's criticism of the simpler version of cultural relativism remains; his view is that it is untenable to argue that the moral values of an individual or a group need not be required to answer to independent criteria of reason.[19] He illustrates his concern using the words of the Italian fascist and wartime prime minister, Benito Mussolini:

> Everything I have said or done in these last years is relativism by intuition. From the fact that all ideologies are of equal value, that all ideologies are mere fictions, the relativist infers that everybody has the right to create for himself his own ideology and to attempt to enforce it with all the energy of which he is capable. If relativism signifies contempt for fixed categories and men who claim to be the bearers of an objective, immortal truth, then there is nothing more relativistic than fascism.[20]

There is no concern here with the question of the soundness of one's moral evaluations or judgements, since the truth or justification of one's ideology and the moral judgments attached to them is not in any way objective, but rather they are relative to the moral standard of some person (or group of persons). As Baghramian and Carter put it, "truth and falsity, right and wrong, standards of reasoning, and procedures of justification are products of differing conventions and frameworks of assessment and . . . their authority is confined to the context giving rise to them".[21]

In fact, relativism is an unconvincing response to the problems of moral disagreement and to calls for tolerance. Firstly, it dismisses or fails to recognise the considerable empirical evidence for moral agreement across different cultures. A number of theorists have argued that the Universal Declaration of Human Rights and the binding covenants and conventions to which it has given rise are indications of significant moral agreement across cultures; other theorists have argued for the existence of a minimal universal morality or a common morality.[22] Secondly and on the other hand, Coady has argued that cultural relativism "involves a simplistic treatment of cultures as wholly unified entitites, ignoring the diversity of moral outlooks within even the simplest cultures".[23] He goes on to conclude that in doing so, cultural relativism makes the possibility of moral advance and reform incoherent; given criticism that relativism dismisses both agreement and disagreement among different cultures, Coady's conclusion is cogent. Thirdly, relativism is impotent in the face of any need to adjudicate between the contrasting moral beliefs or views of different cultures or individuals. There is no external or objective stance that can be adopted to allow us to make moral assessments cross-culturally; and there is no call upon advocates of competing views to subject their views to investigation on the basis of independent criteria of reason, as noted above. Consequently, relativism fails to provide us with a civic minimum that might help us adjudicate between differing moral commitments in pluralistic societies.

Finally, and most relevantly for the purposes of this essay, relativism does not provide logical support for a commitment to tolerance. The existence of competing moral views or schemas, simpliciter, does not imply that those who hold differing views should accept or at least put up with a differing view on the basis of an assertion that the views of all groups are equally deserving of respect. Certainly, as Nussbaum suggests, respect for human beings requires an acknowledgment that there are many different religious and secular ways of life, but such acknowledgement neither implies nor entails tolerance for all moral views, the moral equivalence of all moral views or the impotence of reason in the face of a call to adjudicate between competing moral views.

The final section of this essay considers the factors that might contribute positively both to debate on moral disagreement and to the protection of religious freedom in the Australian public square. In discussing advocacy for tolerance, Coady suggests that such advocacy for tolerance "requires resort to subtle and complex reasoning and insight that goes beyond parochial standards".[24] Coady's comment provides confirmation of a productive approach to questions about moral disagreement, tolerance and the role of religiously informed argument in the public square; it implicitly signals the network of considerations that must come into play if interlocutors in the public space are to manage moral disagreement well. As noted above, these considerations have both philosophical and practical elements. There are a number of conditions that must apply to any objection to the moral views or practices of others. From the philosophical perspective, the objection must be based on good reasons; it cannot simply be a matter of prejudice, bias or hatred. The agent must also have well-justified and non-arbitrary reasons for voluntarily putting up with the objectionable belief or practice. Those reasons may include, as Brennan has suggested, the fact that the objectionable moral view conflicts with the agent's well-formed conscience; it may also conflict with a commitment to upholding particular rights and/or it may have consequences that the agent judges to be deleterious or vicious to individuals or to the social fabric.

Certainly, it must be acknowledged that tolerance has its limits; one cannot be expected to tolerate the intolerable and the limit is identified as the point at which the reasons for bearing objectionable views or practices are outweighed by well-justified reasons for rejecting them. The limits of toleration are justified by our commitments to our foundational and religious beliefs, which are in turn crucial to the maintenance of integrity, both as regards the value of possessing a character that determines that we are "reluctant to abandon or compromise moral principles or ideals" as well as in regard to "a concomitant and more personal sense of self-integration, in which we might identify enduring aspects of ourselves".[25] The call for compromise within political debate can have the unnerving effect of undermining moral principles and ideals, but at the same time, and as Coady points out, while there is a hint of moral danger in compromise, "someone who can seldom or never adjust their policies, projects, or hopes to the desires interest and contrary plans of those they must work with suffers from a defect of character."[26]

The maintenance of integrity is a commitment to practical reasonableness in the conduct of life and, as such, even in cases in which we believe we have well-justified reasons for rejecting views and practices we find objectionable, we are nonetheless not relieved of the responsibility to be reasonable in our interactions with interlocutors. In fact, Brennan's suggestion that prudence and political savvy are crucial within the context of moral disagreement about the role of religion in civic life and in contributing to the development of law and policy,[27] might be bolstered by the addition of a call for the exercise of practical wisdom.

Given concerns, such as Dyson Heydon's, about religious intolerance and discrimination on the basis of religion, attention to a philosophical conception of reasonable tolerance is requisite to ensuring a role for religiously informed argument in public debate. But from the practical perspective, other considerations come into play for the prudent and practically wise agent wishing to help preserve or to enlarge the space in which religiously informed arguments can be prosecuted. Such agents must develop skills requisite to dealing with the fraught nature of this space, referred to above in the discussion of Brennan's views. These practical skills include the capacity to articulate views clearly and sensitively, to be prudent about the way in which a view that others may (perhaps unthinkingly) assume is objectionable is articulated. Consideration of the right way and the right time at which to voice one's view requires attention to the realities of political practice, such as demands for compromise in politics and the utilitarian calculus that often guides political decision-making; it also requires recognition of public mistrust of church statements and church authorities, particularly in the wake of the Royal Commission into Institutional Responses to Child Sexual Abuse and churches' involvement in the scandals that led to the establishment of the Commission.

In summary, what is being recommended in this essay is an approach to political debate in a pluralistic liberal democracy that preserves an open and fruitful—if fraught—space for debate on contentious issues, and one that is particularly committed to the inclusion of religiously informed argument. This approach aims to enrich, rather than impoverish public debate. It recognises the challenges of operating in this space, the potential threat that compromise presents to the maintenance of integrity, and the fact that there are limits to well-justified tolerance. It calls not simply on the goodwill of interlocutors, but also on the use of imagination and curiosity in attempting—as a civic minimum—to come to an understanding of perspectives other than their own.

11

Courtesy, Reason and Legal Education

Catherine Renshaw

Dyson Heydon provides us with an accurate and depressing diagnosis of the malaise affecting contemporary Australian society. He identifies a modern tyrannical elite whose self-absorption and arrogance threatens individual liberties, norms of civility and the principle of equality. He points to the symptoms of the disease: confusion, social decay and violence. He does not explain the cause of the disease, but others have pointed to the moral and intellectual uncertainty that allows intolerance to flourish.[1]

Heydon also, thankfully, refers us to the remedy for the disorder. The remedy, he says, is courtesy and reason. My aim in this reflection is to examine the place of courtesy and reason in the education of law students and to sketch the contribution that education can make to curing some of the evils described by Heydon. My aim is also to address a more difficult question: if there is a place for courtesy and reason in our universities, then how—practically—do we teach these? We are in a world of online lectures, twitter-style pedagogy, edutainment, limited attention spans, frenetic and facile modes of communication. How can teachers impart moderation, reflectiveness, civility and patience?

In 1987, the Pearce Report recommended that no further law schools be established—except possibly for one additional school in Queensland.[2] There were, at the time, 19 law schools in Australia. Since the publication of the Pearce Report, a further 23 law schools have been established in Australian universities.[3] Together, they produce around 7,500 law graduates each year, about half of whom seek to enter the legal profession.[4] The large number of law graduates has been the subject of some excitement in the media around the question of whether the tertiary sector is producing more law graduates than the profession

133

can employ.[5] Nonetheless, demand for studying law remains strong. Law graduates have a better chance of securing employment post-graduation than graduates from other disciplines. Their starting salaries are higher. If they do not become solicitors or barristers, then they end up as in-house counsel for corporations, on the boards of companies, in our parliaments, in the public service, working as policy advisors, in the not-for-profit sector, or in a range of commercial enterprises.

The expansion in the number of law schools has radically altered the socio-economic profile of the typical law student. It is no longer the case that law students mostly come from privileged backgrounds and from private and religious schools.[6] In many law schools, it is not uncommon to have law students who are the first in their family to go to university or whose parents were born overseas. We know some of the practical challenges many of these students face during the period of their degree: limited familiarity with the university habitus; substantial paid work commitments; excessive daily travel time; care responsibilities.[7]

As to the psyche, character and temperament of contemporary law students, many possess the same traits that law students have always possessed. They are, on the whole, ambitious, conformist, competitive and idealistic. More broadly, as Heydon points out, they belong to a largely prosperous generation "for whom the sensual pleasures of the world are freely available." They have not experienced war; they are not hungry; they have not had family members die of preventable diseases. Like their fellow students from other disciplines, the lives of many law students appear to be relatively free of travails and physical hardships. Access to tertiary education is viewed as a right. Smartphones, laptops and the ability to access a vast amount of information instantly are also viewed as fundamental human requirements. The way students learn is profoundly different from the way learning occurred even a decade ago. Understanding is less an individual act of abstract reasoning and logic than a collaborative experience involving navigation, discovery, judgement and creation: *bricolage* rather than deduction.[8]

For young people, the benefits of the digital age—increased connectivity, the fast pace of technological change, accessibility of information, globalization, increased opportunities for innovation and entrepreneurship—come at a cost. They see, in graphic detail and while they are still very young, global problems too numerous to recount: environmental destruction; the suffering of children; the abuse of power by the strong. Before they have had time to properly digest the history of the twentieth century, they realise that their parents and grandparents learnt nothing from it. There are still wars for ideology, pogroms and genocides.[9] Through the internet they are constantly made aware of the fragility of life and the impermanence of meaning. The initial response of young people is to rage and to question. It is not that they do not ask precisely the kinds of questions that Heydon refers to: "What is the nature of humanity?" and "What is the destiny of humanity?"; it is that they ask these questions at too early an age. The answers that are on hand cannot satisfy their hunger for truth and need for hope.

Many young people, before they get as far as university, have arrived at one of two answers to such questions. The first stems from the philosophy of postmodernism, which pervades their education. From this, they learn that these questions about meaning are pointless because there is no objectively true answer to them. A logical response is to turn inward towards indulgence and self-regard. The songs of today's young people are full of descriptions about this process. There is emptiness; there is a search for something; there is nothing at the end of the search; they decide it is pointless continuing to look. They are stressed out; they want to retreat into the helplessness of childhood;[10] they feel deprived.[11] Or if there is something, then it is a wretchedly small answer when set against the large questions of existence: "We've seen it all," sing the Killers, "bonfires of trust, flash-floods of pain," but "it doesn't really matter don't you worry it will all work out."[12] Or in the words of pop superstar Harry Styles: "Just stop your crying and have the time of your life."[13]

The other answer that presents itself is to turn to identity: to find truth and belonging in racial, religious, ethnic, social, or cultural identity. The novelist Ian McEwan describes it well in his novel, *Nutshell*:

> Here's a new politics in university life . . . a strange mood has
> seized the almost educated young. They're on the march, angry
> at times, but mostly needful, longing for authority's blessing,

its validation of their chosen identities. The decline of the west in new guise perhaps. Or the exaltation and liberation of the self. . . . If my identity is that of a believer, I'm easily wounded, my flesh torn to bleeding by any questioning of my faith. Offended, I enter a state of grace. Should inconvenient opinions hover near me like fallen angels or evil djinn (a mile being too near), I'll be in need of the special campus safe room equipped with Play-Doh and looped footage of gamboling puppies. Ah, the intellectual life! I may need advance warning if upsetting books or ideas threaten my very being by coming too close, breathing on my face, my brain, like unwholesome dogs.

I'll feel, therefore I'll be. Let poverty go begging and climate change braise in hell. Social justice can drown in ink. I'll be an activist of the emotions, a loud, campaigning spirit fighting with tears and sighs to shape institutions around my vulnerable self. My identity will be my precious, my only true possession, my access to the only truth. The world must nourish, love and protect it as I do. If my college does not bless me, validate me and give me what I need, I'll press my face into the vice chancellor's lapels and weep. Then demand his resignation.[14]

Identity politics permits the young to deflect questions about right or wrong, the nature of justice, morality, or law. What is right is what they are and how they feel.

Below the surface of what Dyson Heydon sees as an indulged and indulgent generation, a more complicated and troubling picture of modern youth emerges. They are a generation wracked with mental illness.[15] An astonishing number of them starve themselves, cut themselves or kill themselves. They cannot control the world around them, so they control their own bodies in terrible and harmful ways. Their lives lack emotions they can trust, so they hurt themselves to feel something. And, for too many, finding no convincing answer to the question of what it all means, they end their lives. Intellectual and moral confusion is written upon the flesh of our youth. It is not possible to speak to a young person today and find someone who has not been touched by this kind of tragedy. They may have material wealth, but their lives unravel in devastating ways.

Among law students, the prevalence of mental illness is particularly high.[16] If students escape mental illness during the period in which they are at law school, many face it at some point when they leave. The level of depression, stress, family breakdown, drug and alcohol abuse in the legal profession is notable.[17]

Both Australian and American studies have found that law students evince no sign of elevated psychological distress before they enter law school.[18] Legal educators in Australia and elsewhere have begun to ask whether there is something about the study of law, and the environment in which it is taught and practiced, which contributes to stress, anxiety and depression. One hypothesis is that law students learn in an environment that is inevitably competitive, and which perhaps does not reflect the serving aspects of human endeavour which first resonated with some of them, and that this leads to disillusionment or cynicism—a fertile environment for despair.[19] Another theory concerns the way law is taught. At some law schools, for example, students are taught very early on that the law should be approached critically; that it is a tool in the service of the powerful; that it is not the answer they might have thought it was to issues of injustice and inequality. Students are taught to remain detached and not to trust feelings of empathy and compassion. The best marks go to the essays that reflect adversarialism and neutrality. It is of course necessary to emphasise objectivity and critical thinking, particularly to a generation steeped in the virtues of subjectivity. As Professor Terry Tobin QC reminded me, *audi alteram partem* is a fundamental principle of justice—and it is also a cast of mind, an attitude of openness to the possibility of learning from those who hold different positions to our own. The question for the law teacher is how to explain, to a suspicious and jaded generation of students who possess little sense of history, that objectivity does not mean nihilism and the meaning and nature of fundamental moral values that underpin the common law. How can this be done?

One of the first questions new law students consider, when they are taught the very basic structure of the Westminster system of government, is the nature of parliament's power to make laws and the question of what power, if any, the courts have to control parliament.

The student is directed to the decision of Sir Edward Coke in 1609 and his famous words in *Dr Bonham's case*: "the common law will control Acts of Parliament, and sometimes adjudge them to be utterly void; for when an Act of Parliament is against common right and reason, or repugnant, or impossible to be performed, the common law will control it and adjudge such Act to be void."[20] The student is asked to think about what "common right and reason" might mean and is guided towards an understanding of this by considering the facts of *Dr Bonham's case* itself. Dr Bonham was forbidden to practice his profession in London by the Royal College of Physicians unless he first secured its license. Dr Bonham refused. In response, the College first fined him and then imprisoned him, in both instances acting under a royal charter expressly confirmed by an Act of Parliament. In due course, Dr Bonham sued the College for false imprisonment. Is it right and fair (the law student is asked) that Parliament should give the College the power to act as a judge in its own cause, putting people on trial, imposing fines and imprisoning people? Or should parliament, elected by the people and with legitimacy bestowed upon it by democratic processes, have the right to pass any laws it wishes?

The response from students is almost always to side with Sir Edward Coke and Dr Bonham. Students are yet to encounter Dicey and the concept of parliamentary sovereignty; they are excited about their profession and what they hope might be its power to curb the excesses of parliament. Then from the more thoughtful students come the questions: "but how do we know (objectively) what 'common right and reason' is? How do judges know? Don't we (and judges) need to have a shared view about what is good—for us and for society?" These questions are troubling for students, because outside of religion, they have for the most part learned—through the cacophony of voices that make up their worldview—that there is no objective human good, because to affirm otherwise would be to deny significance to the only value about which there is certainty—freedom of choice as an expression of personality.

The teacher of first-year law students at this point has a choice. She can turn the question to the common law idea of reason, perhaps by connecting the statement in *Dr Bonham's case* to Coke's other statements on reason: "reason is the life of the law, nay the common law itself is nothing else but reason, which is to be understood as an artificial perfection of reason, gotten by long study, observation and experience, and not of every man's natural reason."[21] The teacher is on safe ground then, moving the discussion to *legal* reason and reasoning: precedent, induction and deduction, argument by analogy, logic and analysis, the elimination of extraneous facts, the inclusion of relevant material. This is the narrow idea of reason; "artificial" reasoning.[22] It is rational, logical, analytical and dispassionate.

Or, the teacher can turn the discussion to *practical* reason. This is by far the more difficult enterprise. But I suggest that it is impossible to explain legal reason fully and properly without also explaining practical reason. Practical reason leads us to consider the fundamental principles that should direct our actions and guide our lives.

For today's youth, much of their learning is situated in the social and the concrete. One way of explaining practical reason is by engaging the student in a series of questions about the very activity they are doing—learning. Why are you at university? The student's answer is usually something along the lines of: "so that we can learn—gain the knowledge we need to be able to get a job, function in society with confidence, make good decisions based on reality rather than mistakes and deceptions, earn an income and have a good life. That is why we study our books and listen to your lectures." From this, the student understands that knowledge is desirable, a benefit and a good to be pursued.[23] They also understand that the opposite of knowledge—ignorance and confusion—has negative consequences for their lives. So the aim of attaining knowledge is something that should—normatively—direct the student's actions.

Without too much difficulty, one can lead the student to think about other foundational principles that are relevant to students' lives: perhaps friendship; human life; health. And then one can ask the student to reflect on the means they might use to achieve these objectively good things. Should they do *whatever it takes* to maintain friendship, or knowledge, or health? The answer (hopefully) is 'no.' There are multiple goods, and ruthlessly pursuing a single one might jeopardise the ability to achieve other goods: for example, if you study single-mindedly to acquire knowledge it may be to the detriment of your health. And then you might lead the student to consider what is required for the future well-being and fulfilment of others and the need for reciprocal respect. This might mean pursuing goods reasonably, or being reasonable—reflective and conscious about how your pursuit of goods has consequences for yourself and others. Reasonableness can then also be identified as a foundational first principle of practical reason.

At this point, the more impatient students usually interject: they came to law school to learn how to be a lawyer, not a philosopher; how does knowledge of practical reason help them to run a case in court, or advise a client on the law?

The answer to this question is that in arguing a case in court a lawyer often finds herself employing a very different kind of language from that of legal logic. Lawyers argue about just or unjust consequences inherent in proposed solutions. They lead evidence or cross-examine, not merely with a view to establishing matters of fact, but in order to introduce matters pointing to certain degrees of moral fault or innocence, the needs of society and the common good.

In 1992, Professor Garth Nettheim walked into my first-year lecture at the University of New South Wales and, with trembling hands, gave every member of the class a copy of the decision of the High Court of Australia in *Mabo (No. 2)*. "This will change everything," he said, and then he read aloud the words of Justice Brennan:

> A common law doctrine founded on unjust discrimination in the enjoyment of civil and political rights demands reconsideration. It is contrary both to international standards and to the fundamental values of our common law to entrench a discriminatory rule which, because of the supposed position on the scale of social organisation of the indigenous inhabitants of a settled colony, denies them a right to occupy their traditional lands.[24]

Months after the Mabo decision was handed down, our politicians made sure we knew this. Paul Keating stood in Redfern Park and called for:

Recognition that it was we who did the dispossessing. We took the traditional lands and smashed the traditional way of life. We brought the diseases. The alcohol. We committed the murders. We took the children from their mothers. We practised discrimination and exclusion. It was our ignorance and our prejudice. And our failure to imagine these things being done to us. With some noble exceptions, we failed to make the most basic human response and enter into their hearts and minds. We failed to ask—how would I feel if this were done to me? As a consequence, we failed to see that what we were doing degraded all of us.[25]

This was how, to a first-year class of law students, Professor Nettheim sowed the seeds of the idea that reason is not only *legal* reason, or rationality. The law needs to be objective and neutral, but it must also be wise and compassionate. Students begin to sense, even if they have not yet read the cases and decisions that support this idea, that "the measure of the civilization of a society is the extent to which it provides for the needs of the disabled (and of other minorities) and protects them from adverse and unjust discrimination which offends their human dignity."[26] That they need not abandon their deeper quest for meaning, or resign themselves to despair and nihilism.

Courtesy is the second aspect of the remedy proposed by Heydon. In our classrooms, as in our communities, the discussion of difficult legal and moral issues (for example, how to balance individual freedom with the claims of public morality; or personal liberty with the demand of public security; or religious freedom with conflicting social values) has the potential to disintegrate into aggression and personal attacks on those proposing certain views. Criticism of a particular viewpoint is perceived as criticism of the identity of the person who holds that view; and often, the identity of their families and communities. Defensiveness and a propensity to counter-attack is the natural response. At its extreme, the result is the kind of violence Heydon describes: exhortations to "Crucify No Voters" in the marriage debate; or "Burn Churches, Not Gays."

The solution proposed by Heydon is courtesy. Courtesy is not *manners*, or *etiquette*; it is something larger than this.[27] Courtesy is closer to respect—to behaving in a way that is conscious of the effect of your behaviour on others and demonstrating consideration for others and their feelings. Respect requires the ability to see and make contact with other people, and know something of their moral and cultural nature. It requires insight into and understanding of the perspective of others, which can become the platform for a deeper empathy. It requires that we look outward from ourselves to the reality of persons beyond. Philosophers from Adam Smith to Amartya Sen have exhorted us to "go beyond the anchors that seem to fix us to the world in which we live" and understand things in a way that is not moored solely in our own experiences.[28]

Legal educators think hard about how to teach students to understand things in a way that is not moored solely in our own experiences. The difficulty is that at its highest point—the point at which I argue courtesy belongs—what is required is an act of imagination. It begins with our asking Paul Keating's question: "how would I feel if this were done to me?"

Consider a quotidian issue common in the life of a law school: complaints from lecturers about students who do not attend class or who come ill-prepared; complaints from students about lecturers who are overly critical and unsympathetic to the realities of student's lives. For the most part these kinds of animosities bubble along under the surface, but sometimes they spring up in ways that invite the attention of the deputy head of a law school: lecturers storm out of class; students post abusive comments about the lecturer on Facebook. What is lacking in these unpleasant and uncivil interactions is imagination. Has the lecturer thought about what this student's life is like? What it is like, perhaps, to be the first in her family to go to university and to face daily resistance about her choice to study from her parents and peers; about the distance the student travels to get to university; about the fact that her being there means no one is at home to pick up her younger sibling from school, because both her parents are working; about the student's job stacking shelves at the local supermarket at night and about her manager's hint that unless she takes the shifts that clash with her lecture times she will not be offered other shifts; about the pressure to secure an unpaid internship so that she has a chance at securing a job after she graduates; about what it feels like, after overcoming the huge practical hurdles to get to class, to face a lecturer who compounds her self-doubt by criticising her inadequate preparation and questioning her ability ever to join the profession?

Courtesy at its strongest is acknowledging the history and the capacities for joy and pain in another person. We cannot 'reason' our way to this acknowledgement. We need imagination and, I would argue, we need emotion. For those of us born before or on the cusp of the digital age, it was literature that gave us this. Books allow us to enter the experience of another and make it our own; to feel another's anguish and share their joy. If we can do these things then we are well on the way to empathy. If you empathise with someone it is difficult to treat them with discourtesy. You may disagree with them passionately and even dislike them. But it is impossible to summon up vitriol. Could you really scrawl "Crucify No Voters" on the walls of a church after you have read *A Burnt Out Case* or *The End of the Affair*, or any of the complex agonising books in which Graham Greene unravels the heart and conscience of a Catholic? Who could read the *Ballad of Reading Gaol* without burning with the injustice of a society that makes some kinds of love unlawful? Literature shows us that reason can be combined with emotion—with desire and love and the hundred other conditions of the spirit with which writers acquaint us. Dostoevsky said it most clearly: "Don't you see: reason is a fine thing, gentlemen, there's no doubt about it, but it's only reason, and it satisfies only man's rational faculty, whereas desire is a manifestation of all life, that is, of all human life, which includes both reason, as well as all of life's itches and scratches. And although in this manifestation life often turns out to be fairly worthless, it's life all the same, and not merely the extraction of square roots."[29]

The slow digestion of great works of literature is not to the taste of most students today. Reading books does not easily lend itself to multiprocessing; to attention spans which are, on average, between thirty seconds and five minutes. For teachers, the answer is either to despair of the young of today and the age that bred them; or to find a new path to teaching courtesy. Paths do exist. The virtual dimension of online contexts offers students opportunities to engage and experiment with

143

complex, creative, emotionally rich spaces. Using tools they are already expert in, students can explore other and multiple personal identities; experience different possibilities; and do this reflexively in a dialogic medium as part of a collaborative community of learning. All this is difficult to replicate offline. The potential to stimulate the imaginative empathy of the young in the digital age is immense. Yet we teachers seem shuttered in by the Victorian legacy of education: face-to-face lecturing and performative frameworks that reward only individuals.

As a teacher, working in a publicly funded institution which is dedicated to the pursuit of truth and love, Dyson Heydon's words have resonance. Our students are atheists, Muslims, Jews and Christians. On the first day of semester, in the first class, I tell first-year students that there are two principles which our law school insists upon. The first is that everyone is entitled to respect (because they are equal) and that this should manifest itself in courtesy to others and to their views. The second is that everyone has potential to engage in reason, which it is the duty of his or her educators to help him or her realise. These principles underpin the role of the educator within every university. They are at the front and centre of our minds in the law school at Australian Catholic University.

Law school should be a place of searching and creativity in the quest for truth and justice. If it is not, then it is nothing more than a trade school and it hardly deserves to occupy space on a university campus. It is difficult to teach, and almost impossible to test, aspects of the legal profession such as imagination, empathy, self-awareness, and sensitivity to others. For many teachers, the traditional classroom was a more auspicious theatre for learning these things than an online lecture learning experience. In the classroom, at least, we could model the principles of reasoning and courtesy. I would argue, however, that it is still possible to teach these things in a way that our students respond to—regardless of whether they are sitting on a train, at the beach, on their coffee-break, with their earphones in and a small blue screen flashing in front of them.

CONTRIBUTORS

Frank Brennan SJ AO is the CEO of Catholic Social Services Australia and an adjunct professor of law at Australian Catholic University.

Michael Casey is the director of the PM Glynn Institute at Australian Catholic University.

Michael Crennan QC practised at the Victorian Bar for 24 years and has taught in three Austalian universities including Australian Catholic University, where he designed, taught, and was the national co-ordinator of Comparative Legal Systems.

Anne Henderson AM is the deputy director of the Sydney Institute.

Paul Kelly is the editor-at-large of *The Australian*.

Peter Kurti is a senior research fellow with the Culture, Prosperity & Civil Society program at the Centre for Independent Studies, and also adjunct associate professor in the School of Law at the University of Notre Dame Australia.

Sandra Lynch is professor of moral philosophy at the Institute for Ethics and Society, University of Notre Dame Australia.

Shireen Morris is a Mckenzie postdoctoral fellow at Melbourne Law School and senior adviser to Cape York Institute.

Michael Ondaatje is a professor of history and head of the National School of Arts at Australian Catholic University.

Hayden Ramsay is the professor of Catholic philosophy and Pro Vice-Chancellor assisting the Vice-Chancellor and President at Australian Catholic University.

Catherine Renshaw is an associate professor and deputy head of the Thomas More Law School at Australian Catholic University.

Endnotes

Religious 'toleration' in modern Australia: the tyranny of relativism

[1] J.H. Huizinga, *The Waning of the Middle Ages*, transl. edn (Penguin Books Ltd, 1922), p. 1.

[2] P. Kurti, *The Tyranny of Tolerance* (Connor Court Publishing, 2017), p. 6.

[3] Quoted in L. Siedentop, *Inventing the Individual* (Allen Lane, 2014), p. 118.

[4] *Ibid*, p. 96.

[5] Galatians 3:28.

[6] Siedentop, *op. cit.*, p. 353.

[7] *Ibid*.

[8] *Ibid*, p. 77.

[9] *Ibid*, p. 80.

[10] *Ibid*, p. 89.

[11] *Muhur v Ashcroft*, 355 F 3d 958 at 961 (7th Cir, 2004).

[12] *International Convention on the Elimination of All Forms of Racial Discrimination* (1965), article 1(1).

[13] However, section 56 does provide that nothing in the Act affects the ordination of priests, the training of priests, the appointment of other persons by religious bodies and any other act or practice of a religious body that conforms to the doctrines of the religion or is necessary to avoid injury to the religious susceptibilities of the adherents of that religion.

[14] *Christian Youth Camps Ltd v Cobaw Community Health Service Ltd* (2014) 50 VR 256; [2014] VSCA 75.

[15] P. Mulherin and S.P. Kennedy, "Archipelago or Landmass? Voluntary Associations, Civil Society and the Health of Liberal Democracy", *Policy*, Vol. 33, issue 2 (2017), p. 40.

1. A history of respectful debate

[1] *Official Records of the Debates of the Australasian Federal Convention*, Adelaide, 1897, p. 1184.

[2] Quoted by G. O'Collins, *Patrick McMahon Glynn* (Melbourne University Press, 1965), p. 139.

[3] Clause 16 of Chapter V (States): see *Official Records of the Debates of the Australasian Federal Convention*, Sydney, 1891, p. 962. It was not discussed at the 1891 Sydney Convention. It was retained unamended in the 1897 draft as clause 109: see *Official Records of the Debates of the Australasian Federal Convention*, Adelaide, 1897, p. 124, having been agreed to without discussion at p. 1004 on 20 April 1897.

[4] *Official Records of the Debates of the Australasian Federal Convention*, Adelaide, 1897, p. 1186.

[5] *Ibid*.

[6] *Ibid*.

[7] *Ibid*, p. 1187.

[8] *Ibid*, p. 1188.

[9] *Ibid*, p. 1189.

[10] *Official Records of the Debates of the Australasian Federal Convention*, Melbourne, 1898, p. 658.

[11] *Ibid*, p. 654.

[12] *Ibid*, p. 661.

[13] *Ibid*.

[14] *Ibid*, p. 664.

[15] *Ibid*, p. 1732.

[16] *Ibid*, p. 1733.

[17] *Ibid*, p. 1734.

[18] *Ibid*.

[19] *Church of the Holy Trinity* v *United States*, 143 US 457 (1892), at 471.

[20] *Official Records of the Debates of the Australasian Federal Convention*, Melbourne, 1898, p. 1734.

[21] *Ibid*, p. 1735.

[22] *Ibid*, p. 1737.

[23] *Ibid*, p. 1738.

[24] *Ibid*, p. 1769.

[25] Quoted in O'Collins, *op. cit.*, p. 143.

[26] *Official Records of the Debates of the Australasian Federal Convention*, Melbourne, 1898, p. 2515.

[27] Final Report of the Constitutional Commission, 1988, Volume 1, p. 105.

[28] *Ibid*, p. 110.

[29] Report of the Constitutional Convention, Transcript of Proceedings, Volume 1, 2 February 1998, p. 11.

[30] *Ibid*.

[31] Report of the Constitutional Convention, Transcript of Proceedings, Volume 3, 1998, p. 426.

[32] *Ibid*, p. 427.

[33] *Ibid*.

[34] *Ibid*, p. 429.

[35] *Ibid*, p. 430.

[36] *Ibid*, p. 486.

[37] *Ibid*, p. 527.

[38] *Ibid*, p. 648; motion carried at p. 651.

4. Reasons to fear war

[1] V. Orbán, Speech at the 29th Bálványos Summer Open University and Student Camp, 28 July 2018, Tusnádfürdő (Băile Tuşnad), http://abouthungary.hu/speeches-and-remarks/prime-minister-viktor-orbans-speech-at-the-29th-balvanyos-summer-open-university-and-student-camp/.

[2] C. Fox, "The Dangers of Illiberal Liberalism", *The Economist*, 17 August 2018. https://www.economist.com/open-future/2018/08/17/the-dangers-of-illiberal-liberalism.

[3] *Ibid*. See also M. Lilla, "The End of Identity Liberalism", *New York Times*, 18 November 2016, https://www.nytimes.com/2016/11/20/opinion/sunday/the-end-of-identity-liberalism.html; K. Franke, "Making White Supremacy Respectable. Again", 21 November 2016, http://blog.lareviewofbooks.org/essays/making-white-supremacy-respectable/.

[4] Fox, *op. cit.*

[5] F. Fukuyama, "Against Identity Politics", *Foreign Affairs*, September-

October 2018, https://www.foreignaffairs.com/articles/americas/2018-08-14/ against-identity-politics.

[6] *Ibid.*

[7] Fox, *op. cit.*

[8] "The Paris Statement: A Europe We Can Believe In" (October 2017), pars 16 & 24, https://thetrueeurope.eu/a-europe-we-can-believe-in/.

[9] A. Pabst, "Democracy's Descent into Demagogy: Prospects for Cultural Renewal in a Post-Truth Age", ABC Religion and Ethics, 9 May 2018, http://www.abc.net.au/religion/articles/2018/05/09/4841000.htm.

[10] D. Farrow, "Freedom of Conscience and Religion: A Casualty of the Autonomy Doctrine", 15 March 2017, p. 15, https://www.cardus.ca/research/law/reports/freedom-of-conscience-and-religion/.

5. A fundamental right under threat

[1] N. Tabakoff, "Israel Folau: The Right to Speak Freely", *The Australian*, 10 April 2018.

[2] Article 2(1) of the ICCPR states: "Each State Party to the present Covenant undertakes to respect and to ensure to all individuals within its territory and subject to its jurisdiction the rights recognised in the present Covenant, without distinction of any kind, such as race, colour, sex, language, religion, political or other opinion, national or social origin, property, birth or other status." I am grateful to Dr Augusto Zimmermann for drawing to my attention the significant role of the former USSR in the drafting of the ICCPR. The USSR brought pressure to bear to secure restriction of speech as a matter of human rights law. In proposing the extension of restraint, the USSR introduced the notion of "incitement to hatred" and thereby helped secure international commitment to the elimination of intolerance. A full account of this can be found in C. Berg, *In Defence of Freedom of Speech* (Institute of Public Affairs, 2012), pp. 171–176.

[3] Even though multiculturalism had yet to emerge as a specific policy objective in 1974 when the bill was before Parliament, debate was conducted in terms of its implications for the notion of a multicultural society. For more on this see M. Lopez, *The Origins of Multiculturalism in Australian Politics, 1945–1975* (Melbourne University Press, 2000), pp. 410–417.

[4] In addition to approximately 12,000 religious organisations that comprise

the largest single group of not-for-profit organisations, a substantial number of religious charities (sometimes known as "faith-based organisations") provide services in education, health, disability and aged care. See the Productivity Commission's 2010 research report, "Contribution of the Not-for-Profit Sector", cited in S. Judd, A. Robinson, and F. Errington, *Driven by Purpose* (Hammond Press, 2012), p. 43.

[5] See the decision of the Supreme Court of Canada in *R v Big M Drug Mart Ltd* [1985] 1 SCR 295, 336 per Dickson J at 94–95.

[6] R. Ahdar and I. Leigh, *Religious Freedom in the Liberal State* (Oxford University Press, 2012), p. 46.

[7] Article 18(1) of the Universal Declaration of Human Rights 1948 states: "Everyone has the right to freedom of thought, conscience and religion; this right includes freedom to change his religion or belief, and freedom, either alone or in community with others and in public or private, to manifest his religion or belief in teaching, practice, worship and observance."

[8] These provisions are set out in Article 18(2) of the ICCPR: "No one shall be subject to coercion which would impair his freedom to have or to adopt a religion or belief of his choice." Article 18(3): "Freedom to manifest one's religion or beliefs may be subject only to such limitations as are prescribed by law and are necessary to protect public safety, order, health, or morals or the fundamental rights and freedoms of others." Article 18(3) was adopted from Article 9(2) of the European Convention on the Protection of Human Rights and Fundamental Freedoms 1950.

[9] The High Court has generally adopted an expansive approach to the construction of "external affairs" so that the external affairs power has been used as a platform to expand federal legislative power. The Commonwealth Parliament has not, thus far, used the external affairs power to create more comprehensive protections for religious freedom.

[10] Section 116 of the Australian Constitution confers no constitutional right to the free expression of religion. It simply places a *limit* on the legislative power of the Commonwealth Parliament and forbids it from imposing a religious qualification for certain kinds of position. Nor does section 116 afford an individual any constitutional right to assert freedom of religion against the actions of other individuals or organisations. Indeed, as Carolyn Evans, a legal scholar, notes, section 116 does not even create a positive obligation for Parliament to protect religious freedom. It simply secures

freedom for the citizen by constraining the power of Parliament: see C. Evans, *Legal Protection of Religious Freedom in Australia* (Federation Press, 2012), p. 73.

[11] *Charter of Human Rights and Responsibilities Act 2006* (Vic) and *Human Rights Act 2004* (ACT).

[12] Section 14 of the Victorian Charter states: "(1) Every person has the right to freedom of thought, conscience, religion and belief, including (a) the freedom to have or to adopt a religion or belief of his or her choice; and (b) the freedom to demonstrate his or her religion or belief in worship, observance, practice and teaching, either individually or as part of a community, in public or in private. (2) A person must not be coerced or restrained in a way that limits his or her freedom to have or adopt a religion or belief in worship, observance, practice or teaching."

[13] Senator Sarah Hanson-Young (Greens, South Australia), for example, has declared that it is not merely outdated to hold that marriage can only be between a man and a woman but extremely defamatory: see "South Australian Premier Mike Rann's call for gay marriage gets support from Liberals", news.com.au (10 October 2011), https://www.news.com.au/national/breaking-news/south-australian-premier-mike-ranns-call-for-gay-marriage-gets-support-from-liberals/news-story/ef0707b96175c34927b5df2b34d00b8a

[14] M.J. Sandel, "Religious Liberty—Freedom of Conscience or Freedom of Choice?", *Utah Law Review* (1989), pp. 597ff, p. 611.

[15] A point well made in R. Blackford, *Freedom of Religion and the Secular State* (Wiley-Blackwell, 2012), p. 11.

[16] P. Parkinson, "Religious Vilification, Anti-Discrimination Laws and Religious Minorities in Australia: The Freedom to Be Different", *Australian Law Journal*, Vol. 81, issue 12 (2007), pp. 954–966, p. 965.

[17] *Ibid*.

[18] P. Parkinson and J. Harrison, "Freedom beyond the Commons: Managing the Tension between Faith and Equality in a Multicultural Society", *Monash University Law Review*, Vol. 40, no. 2 (2014), pp. 413-451, p. 422.

[19] *Ibid*, pp. 442-443.

[20] *Ibid*, p. 444.

[21] *Ibid*, p. 445.

[22] *Ibid*, p. 451.

[23] R. Williams, "Secularism, Faith and Freedom", Lecture delivered at the Pontifical Academy of Social Sciences, Rome (23 November 2006), quoted in Ahdar and Leigh, *op.cit.*, p. 96.

[24] *Ibid*.

[25] R. Plant, "Religion, Identity and Freedom of Expression", *Res Publica*, Vol. 17 (2011), pp. 7-20, p. 8.

[26] See, for example, J. Waldron, *The Harm in Hate Speech* (Harvard University Press, 2012), p. 127.

6. Church-state relations in recent history

[1] See discussion of the DOGS case below.

[2] The last established church survived until 1833, in Massachusetts.

[3] The order is significant, a fact which escaped the Confederate States, with terrible consequences.

[4] 330 US 1.

[5] For the 'Wall of separation' see I. Bertrum, "Of Historiography and Constitutional Principle: Jefferson's Reply to the Danbury Baptists", *Journal of Church and State,* Vol. 51, no.1 (2009), pp. 102-125; D. Dreisbach, "Mr Jefferson, A Mammoth Cheese, and the 'Wall of Separation Between Church and State': a Bicentennial Commemoration", *Journal of Church and State*, Vol. 43, no. 4 (2001), pp. 725-745.

[6] 374 US (1963).

[7] 333 US 203.

[8] *School District of Abington Township v Schempp* 374 US 203.

[9] *Lemon v Kurtzman* 403 US 602.

[10] *Marsh v Chamb*ers 463 US 783.

[11] *Girourard v United States* 328 US (1946).

[12] *Davis v Beason* 133 US 333.

[13] 367 US 488.

[14] 565 US (2012).

[15] 573 US (2014).

[16] Compare the reasoning of the Victorian Court of Appeal in *Christian Youth Camps Limited & Ors v Cobaw Community Health Services Limited & Ors* [2014] VSCA 75 (16 April 2014).

[17] The Court held that "The laws and the Constitution can, and in some cases must, protect gay persons and gay couples in the exercise of their civil rights, but religious and philosophical objections to gay marriage are protected views and in some instances protected forms of expression". In this case, the extravagant language of the Commission from which the appeal was brought was sternly criticized: it described the Christian views of Mr Phillips as "despicable", "merely rhetorical", comparable with "defenses of slavery and the Holocaust". The Court followed earlier authority that "government cannot impose regulations that are hostile to the religious beliefs of affected citizens and cannot act in a manner that passes judgement on or presupposes the illegitimacy of religious beliefs and practices". Whilst in some cases the State's interest may be weighted against sincerely held religious beliefs, the decisions must be considered "with the neutrality required by the Free Exercise clause" which must be "strictly observed". These quotations are taken from pp. 1-3 of the Syllabus (*scil.* headnote) of the Court's decision in *Masterpiece Cakeshop Ltd, et al, Petitioners v Colorado Civil Rights Commission, et al* 584 US (2018).

[18] *Krygger v Williams* (1912) 15 CLR 366.

[19] Per Griffith CJ in sharp contrast to the reasoning later to come in the Hobby Lobby case discussed above.

[20] *Adelaide Company of Jehovah's Witnesses Incorporated v Commonwealth* (1943) 67 CLR 116, per Latham CJ at 1.

[21] *Attorney General (Vic) Ex Rel Black v Commonwealth* (1981) 146 CLR 559.

[22] See discussion of the DOGS case above.

[23] Procedures are laid down in the Act designed to ensure that new legislation will be subject to scrutiny as to its conformity with the Charter. Section 37 provides that "so far as it is possible to do so consistently with their meaning, all statutory provisions must be interpreted in a way that is compatible with human rights". Parliament can make an override declaration which removes proposed legislation from the scrutiny processes set out in the Act.

[24] Perhaps 'possibly' is too tentative. The anti-discrimination commissioner of Tasmania threatened action against Archbishop Porteous arising out of

a complaint that he had circulated 'offensive' material which set out the Church's teaching on same-sex marriage. The significance of this remains hypothetical, because the complaint was withdrawn. It was also brought under one of the strictest regimes of anti-discrimination laws in Australia. It is clearly inconsistent with section14 of the Charter.

9. A warning to conservative elites

[1] See, for example, the old laws preventing non-white people from voting in certain jurisdictions, or the policies mandating unequal wages on the basis of race (e.g. Commonwealth of Australia, *Unfinished Business: Indigenous Stolen Wages report*, 2006; *Bligh and others v State of Queensland* [1996] HREOCA 28), enforcing segregation (the Protection Acts empowered appointed protectors and boards to control many day-to-day aspects of Indigenous people's lives: see e.g. *Aborigines Protection Act 1886* (WA), *Aborigines Protection Act 1869* (Vic), *Aboriginals Preservation and Protection Act 1939* (Qld), and discriminatory immigration under the White Australia Policy.

[2] In some jurisdictions there were laws banning homosexual sex, and women were denied rights to full citizenship on account of their sex.

[3] See N. Earls, "Australia once banned Catholics from mass and vilified the Irish. Haven't we learned anything?", *Guardian,* 22 July 2016.

[4] A Rigney, Kaurna Warra Pintyandi, Committee Hansard, Adelaide, 2 April 2012, p. 1. See www.aphref.aph.gov.au_house_committee__atsia_languages2_report_chapter3.pdf/.

[5] Prior to the 1967 referendum, section 51(xxvi), the race power, explicitly excluded Indigenous people from its operation and section 127 prevented Indigenous people from being counted in the census for the purposes of voting.

[6] Convention delegate James Howe argued that "we should as far as possible make Australia home for Australians and the British race alone" and emphasised the importance of Parliament retaining power to control "coloured persons" in various ways: *Official Record of the Debates of the Australasian Federal Convention*, Melbourne, 28 January 1898, p. 251. See also *Official Record of the Debates of the Australasian Federal Convention*, Third Session, Melbourne, 20 January – 17 March 1898, p. 240.

[7] Christian missions were part of the colonial project and, however viewed, there is a complex relationship between religion and colonialism. See discussion in P. Harrison, "'Fill the Earth and Subdue it': Biblical Warrants for Colonization in Seventeenth Century England" (2005), http://epublications.bond.edu.au/hss_pubs/54.

[8] Such attitudes were also evident in the colonisation of New Zealand. See *Wi Parata v Bishop of Wellington* (1877) 3 NZJur (NS) 72 (SC), 78.

[9] P. Naughtin, "Deakin MP Michael Sukkar abstains from same-sex marriage vote", *Herald Sun,* 8 December 2017.

[10] In 2016, I argued in *The Age* that Australia Day should be the date the nation votes for constitutional recognition, to ensure the injustices of the past will not happen again: S. Morris, "No Australian should feel like a stranger in their own country", *The Age,* 25 January 2016. It should be the day we finally bring together our Indigenous heritage, our British inheritance and our multicultural triumph, and guarantee the First Nations a voice in their affairs. Then it could become a day of broadening, not burning; including and embracing, not repudiating. A comment from a member of the public under my article suggested an efficient solution: why not hold the Indigenous recognition referendum on 26 January? Rather than changing the date, as many progressives argue, why not transform and redeem it? This could be the radical centre solution. With a bit of vision, 26 January could be the date we do that which should have been done in 1788 and 1901: belatedly include a First Nations' voice in the Constitution as the Uluru Statement requests, and bring together the three parts of our nation through a legislated Declaration enacted by all Australian parliaments: the Indigenous, the British and the multicultural. Then 26 January would become a solemn day of historical reconciliation. A day of healing, resolution and peace-making.

[11] P. Kelly, "Barnaby Joyce and the crisis of conservatism in Australia", *The Australian,* 21 February 2018.

[12] N. Pearson, "Conservatives leave door open to progressive change", *The Australian,* 10 March 2018.

10. Relativism, tolerance and morality

[1] Dyson Heydon referred to Siedentop, L., *Inventing the Individual* (Allen Lane, 2014), p. 118.

[2] R. Forst, "Toleration" in E.N. Zalt (ed.), *The Stanford Encyclopedia of Philosophy* (Fall 2017 Edition), <https://plato.stanford.edu/archives/fall2017/entries/toleration/>.

[3] Quoted in M.C. Nussbaum, *The New Religious Intolerance* (Harvard University Press, 2012). Emphasis added.

[4] Forst, *op. cit.*

[5] *Ibid.*

[6] M. Maddox, "Finding God in Global Politics", *International Political Science Review*, Vol. 36, issue 2 (2014), pp. 185–196.

[7] P. Norris and R. Inglehart, *Sacred and Secular*, 2nd edn (Cambridge University Press, 2012), p. 4.

[8] *Ibid*; P.L. Berger (ed.), *The Desecularization of the World* (Ethics and Public Policy Center, 1999).

[9] Nick Cater, for example, finds the question of the truth of religious belief irrelevant and argues that religion's value lies in its capacity to create social cohesion: *The Lucky Culture and the Rise of an Australian Ruling Class* (Harper Collins, 2013).

[10] F. Brennan, "Mixing Law, Religion and Politics", Inaugural Lecture, Institute of Legal Studies, Australian Catholic University, 21 September 2005, http://www.acu.edu.au/__data/assets/pdf_file/0012/10335/ACU_Inaugural_lecture.pdf

[11] *Ibid.*

[12] *Ibid.*

[13] J. Rawls, *Political Liberalism*, 2nd edn (Columbia University Press, 2005); *A Theory of Justice* (Harvard University Press, 1971).

[14] R. Audi, "Moral Foundations of Liberal Democracy, Secular Reasons, and Liberal Neutrality toward the Good", *Notre Dame Journal of Law, Ethics & Public Policy,* Vol. 19, issue 1 (2012).

[15] *Ibid*, p. 216, quoting from Audi, R., *Religious Commitment and Secular Reason* (Cambridge University Press, 2000).

[16] *Ibid*, p. 217.

[17] D. Wong, "Relativism" in P. Singer (ed.), *A Companion to Ethics* (Blackwell Publishers, 1993).

[18] C.A.J. Coady, *Messy Morality* (Oxford University Press, 2008), p. 36.

[19] *Ibid*, p.37.

[20] Quoted in H. Veatch, "A Critique of Benedict" in J.R. Weinberg and K. Yandell (eds), *Problems in Philosophical Inquiry* (Holt, Rinehard and Winston, 1971), p. 27.

[21] M. Baghramian and J.A. Carter, "Relativism" in E.N. Zalta (ed.), *The Stanford Encyclopedia of Philosophy* (Summer 2017 Edition), https://plato. stanford.edu/archives/sum2017/entries/relativism/.

[22] M.C. Nussbaum, "In Defense of Universal Values", Fifth Annual Hesburgh Lectures on Ethics and Public Policy: Women and Development, 1999, http://philosophy.uchicago.edu/faculty/files/nussbaum/In%20Defense%20 of%20Universal%20Values.pdf; S. Alkire, "The Basic Dimensions of Human Flourishing: A Comparison of Accounts" in N. Biggar and R. Black (eds), *The Revival of Natural Law* (Ashgate, 2000), pp. 73-110; J. Haldane, "Ethical Disagreement and the Possibility of a Common Morality", lecture at Ethics Matters Symposium held at Royal Holloway, University of London, 19 November 2001, p. 8. Part of the lecture drew on J. Haldane, *An Intelligent Person's Guide to Religion* (Duckworth, 2003).

[23] Coady, *op. cit.*, p. 37.

[24] *Ibid*, pp. 36-37.

[25] H. Ramsay, *Beyond Virtue* (Macmillan, 1997), p. 3.

[26] Coady, *op. cit.*, p. 45.

[27] *Ibid*.

11. Courtesy, reason and legal education

[1] Lord Hailsham LC, "Reflections on a Remark by Cicero", *Encounter*, Vol. 56 (1981), p. 42.

[2] D. Pearce, E. Campbell and D. Harding, *Australian Law Schools: A Discipline Assessment for the Commonwealth Tertiary Education Commission* (AGPS, 1987).

[3] D. Barker, "An Avalanche of Law Schools: 1989 to 2013", *Journal of the Australasian Law Teachers Association* , Vol. 6 (2013), p. 177.

[4] J. Lee, "Graduates shun legal profession", *The Age*, 20 May 2012.

[5] E. Tadros, "Too many law graduates and not enough jobs", *Australian Financial Review*, 22 October 2015.

[6] M.D. Kirby, "Justice for All", *The Stand*: http://stand.uow.edu.au/michael-kirby-justice-for-all/.

[7] H. Brook, D. Fergie, M. Maeorg and D. Mitchell, *Universities in Transition* (University of Adelaide Press, 2014).

[8] J.S. Brown, "Growing Up Digital: How the Web Changes Work, Education and the Ways People Learn", *Change* (March-April 2000).

[9] E.T. Kennan, "The Moral Functions of Higher Education in Modern Society", *Journal of College and University Law*, Vol. 20, issue 1 (1993), p. 69.

[10] Twenty-one Pilots, "Stressed Out" (2015).

[11] Robbie Williams, "Supreme" (2000).

[12] The Killers, "Exitlude" (2006).

[13] Harry Styles, "Sign of the Times" (2017).

[14] I. McEwan, *Nutshell* (Penguin, 2016), p. 146.

[15] Mission Australia's 2016 Youth Survey found that almost a quarter (22.8 per cent) of young people aged 15 to 19 show the symptoms of probable serious mental illness; and that teenage girls were more than twice as likely as boys to be in severe psychological distress, even though the suicide rate was higher in males. The three top stressors for teens were: coping with stress; school and study problems; and depression. Other notable issues were bullying, family conflict and suicide.

[16] See N. Kelk et al, *Courting the Blues* (Brain & Mind Research Institute: University of Sydney, 2009); N. Kelk, S. Medlow and I. Hickie, "Distress and Depression among Australian Law Students: Incidence, Attitudes and the Role of Universities", *Sydney Law Review*, Vol. 32 (2010), p. 113; K.M. Sheldon and L.S. Krieger, "Understanding the Negative Effects of Legal Education on Law Students: A Longitudinal Test of Self-Determination Theory", *Personality and Social Psychology Bulletin*, Vol. 22 (2007), p. 883; W. Larcombe et al, "Does an Improved Experience of Law School Protect Students against Depression, Anxiety and Stress? An Empirical Study of Wellbeing and the Law School Experience of LLB and JD Students", *Sydney Law Review*, Vol. 35 (2013), p. 407; M.E. Pritchard and D.N. McIntosh, "What Predicts Adjustment among Law Students? A Longitudinal Panel Study", *The Journal of Social Psychology*, Vol. 143 (2003), p. 727; A. Bergin and K. Pakenham, "Law Student Stress: Relationships between Academic

Demands, Social Isolation, Career Pressure, Study/Life Imbalance and Adjustment Outcomes in Law Students", *Psychiatry, Psychology and Law*, Vol. 22, issue 3 (2015). Christine Parker (2014) has pointed out that there are methodological limitations associated with some of the empirical studies because they are based on psychological distress scales but are cited to imply clinical conclusions. The repetition of this flaw in a number of surveys led Parker to conclude that the well-being 'crisis' affecting both law students and practising lawyers was an example of a contemporary 'moral panic': C. Parker, "The 'Moral Panic' over Psychological Wellbeing in the Legal Profession: A Personal or Political Ethical Response?" *University of New South Wales Law Journal*, Vol. 37, Issue 3 (2014), p. 1103.

[17] J. Chan, S. Poynton and J. Bruce, "Lawyering, Stress and Work Culture: an Australian Study", *UNSW Law Journal*, Vol. 37, Issue 3, p. 1062.

[18] A. Lester, L. England and N. Antolak-Saper, "Health and Wellbeing in the First Year: The Law School Experience", *Alternative Law Journal*, Vol. 36 (2011), p. 47.

[19] M.T. O'Brien, S. Tang and K. Hall, "Changing Our Thinking: Empirical Research on Law Student Wellbeing, Thinking Styles and the Law Curriculum", *Legal Education Review*, Vol. 21 (2011), p. 149; W. Larcombe et al, "Does an Improved Experience of Law School Protect Students against Depression, Anxiety and Stress? An Empirical Study of Wellbeing and the Law School Experience of LLB and JD Students", *Sydney Law Review*, Vol. 35 (2013), p. 407.

[20] *Dr. Bonham's Case*, 8 Co. Rep. 114 (Court of Common Pleas) [1610].

[21] E. Coke, *Commentary upon Littleton* 97b (1628), C. Butler (ed.), 18th edn (Legal Classics Library, 1985).

[22] *Prohibitions del Roy* (1607) 12 Co. Rep. 63.

[23] J. Finnis, *Reason in Action* (Oxford University Press, 2011), p. 3.

[24] *Mabo and Ors v Queensland (No 2)* (1992) 175 CLR 1.

[25] P.J. Keating, Redfern Speech (Year for the World's Indigenous People), Redfern Park, 10 December 1992, https://antar.org.au/sites/default/files/paul_keating_speech_transcript.pdf.

[26] *Walters v Public Transport Corporation* (1992) 173 CLR 349, 372 per Brennan J.

[27] I am indebted to Professor Terry Tobin QC for directing me to the

etymology of 'courtesy': from the old French *curteisie, cortoisie*, meaning 'courtliness, noble sentiments, generosity'.

[28] A. Smith, *The Theory of Moral Sentiment* (1759), revised edn (Clarendon Press, 1976), p. 11. Smith's perspective on moral reasoning is discussed in A. Sen, "Open and Closed Impartiality", *Journal of Philosophy*, Vol. 99 (2002), p. 445.

[29] F. Dostoyevsky, *Notes from the Underground*, transl. J. Kentish (Oxford University Press, 1999), p. 28.

Index

www.ingramcontent.com/pod-product-compliance
Lightning Source LLC
Chambersburg PA
CBHW070703190326
41458CB00046B/6831/J